Dion Fortune's
RITES of ISIS
and of PAN

Dion Fortune's
RITES of ISIS and of PAN

edited by
Gareth Knight

SKYLIGHT PRESS

© Gareth Knight & The Society of the Inner Light, 2013

First published in Great Britain in 2013 by Skylight Press,
210 Brooklyn Road, Cheltenham, Glos GL51 8EA

Designed and typeset by Rebsie Fairholm
Publisher: Daniel Staniforth
Cover image by Rebsie Fairholm

www.skylightpress.co.uk

Printed and bound in Great Britain by Lightning Source, Milton Keynes.
Typeset in Adobe Caslon Pro. Titles set in Polyspring, a font by Pintassilgo
Prints.

British Library Cataloguing in Publication Data.
A catalogue record for this book is available from the British Library.

ISBN 978-1-908011-77-0 (paperback)

[Also published in a limited edition hardback: ISBN 978-1-908011-87-9]

CONTENTS

DION FORTUNE, HER RITES AND HER NOVELS

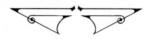

I N 1927, having abandoned a promising career in psychotherapy a decade before, and honed her skills in the various options of the esoteric world, Dion Fortune founded her Fraternity (later Society) of the Inner Light. Progress was rapid, and in the Spring of 1930 a new phase of the work was announced. The three degrees of a Lesser Mystery system were now working and they planned to open a Threshold Degree leading to the celebration of the Greater Mysteries. This expansion of the work brought about a considerable development in Dion Fortune herself, and thence to the group and the wider world.

It began with a partial withdrawal from organising and lecturing to concentrate more upon inner work, which after a series of powerful experiences[1] led to her writing *The Mystical Qabalah*. It appeared as monthly instalments in *The Inner Light Magazine* from 1931 through 1934, was published in 1935 by Williams and Norgate, and remains to this day, several publishers later and never out of print, an important user-friendly textbook on the Qabalistic foundations of the Western Esoteric Tradition.

However, despite this considerable achievement, she was not entirely satisfied, and set about writing a series of novels in which she sought to give examples of the Qabalah in practice, particularly through the power of ritual. For as she later remarked, in an article of 1936, *"to know the Mystery system is one thing; to know how to make it work*

---

1 For an example of a Qabalistic vision see Appendix 3.

is another... Because of the difficulties attending the expression of it, there is much more of it to be found in my novels than in my other books; for in the novels it can be present in pictorial form, which has always been the method of the Mysteries for the excellent reason that it is the only possible one ...."

The novels to which she referred are *The Winged Bull* (1935), *The Goat-Foot God* (1936), and *The Sea Priestess* (1938). She had yet to write *Moon Magic.* Her earlier occult blood and thunder novel *The Demon Lover* (1927) and the short stories *The Secrets of Dr. Taverner* (1922) stand apart as early work with different aims in view.[2]

In the later novels she sought to bring about a direct experience of Qabalistic principles to her readers, although she began to have her doubts as to how successful this literary experiment had been, which she discussed in another article – *"The Winged Bull – a study in esoteric psychology"*, in 1938.[3]

But this was not the only string to her bow. In 1936, a "new epoch" was announced in the growth and organisation of the Fraternity, one consequence of which was leasing of an old converted church in Belgravia called "The Belfry". Here she was able to stage her Rite of Isis – and possibly the Rite of Pan – for a public (although probably carefully selected) audience.

Performing rituals in public may seem, by Dion Fortune's own account, hardly the most effective mode of ceremonial magic, for like grand opera and other specialist art forms, it needs a sympathetic and informed audience. Yet it can have its place in certain circumstances. And in this respect she was by no means a trailblazer, for a Rite of Isis had been performed in Paris by the Golden Dawn founders S.L. and Moina MacGregor Mathers in 1899 when Dion Fortune was still a schoolgirl in Weston-super-Mare.

However, Bernard Bromage, a London University lecturer and researcher on oriental esoteric systems, who witnessed her Rite of Isis, was much impressed by it. As he remarked in an article on Dion Fortune (in *Light*, the journal of the College of Psychic Studies, Spring 1960) it remained in his memory *"one of the best attempts I have ever witnessed to stimulate the subconscious by means of 'pantomime' drawn from the more ancient records of the hierophant's art."*

The use of the word 'pantomime' could perhaps have been better

2 See Appendix 2 for her article on *The Novels of Dion Fortune.*
3 See Appendix 3.

chosen, but he was obviously at a loss to describe exactly the nature of the evening's experience, and was using the term in a technical rather than a theatrical sense.

As a result of their mutual respect, Bernard Bromage helped set up a series of Saturday evening lecture/discussions with Dion Fortune in the Autumn of 1937, which featured an impressive panel of visitors, including the novelists Marjorie Bowen, Berta Ruck and Claude Houghton, Christina Foyle of the famous book emporium, and psychical researcher Elliot O'Donnell. They attracted a large and intelligent audience, and as Bernard Bromage later put it, *"threshed out many of the problems which had preoccupied distinguished minds in the field of occult speculation. They made people think, and they came back for more."*

Performances at the Belfry were backed up by illustrated lectures and demonstrations at Dion Fortune's Bayswater headquarters, as may be seen in a lecture programme for Spring 1938, topped and tailed by her husband Dr Thomas Penry Evans before he went off to the Spanish Civil War.

Jan 17: Spiritual Healing: its Power and Limitations, by Dr. T. Penry Evans.

Jan 31: Methods of Occult Training by Dion Fortune and C. R. F. Seymour M.A. with a practical demonstration.

Feb 7: Ceremonial Magic by Dion Fortune.

Feb 14: A Reconstruction of Isis Worship. Part 1. A lantern lecture by C.R.F. Seymour M.A. with chanting by Dion Fortune.

Feb 21: The Esoteric Doctrine of Sex and Polarity, by Dion Fortune.

Feb 28: A Reconstruction of Isis Worship. Part 2. A lantern lecture by C.R.F. Seymour M.A. with chanting by Dion Fortune.

Mar 7: The Doctrine of Magical Images by Dion Fortune.

Mar 14: A Reconstruction of the Worship of Pan. A lantern lecture by C.R.F. Seymour M.A. with chanting by Dion Fortune.

Mar 21: The Mental Factor in Health, by Dr T. Penry Evans.

Colonel C.R.F. Seymour was a senior member of the Fraternity at this time who contributed a number of articles, particularly upon pagan topics, to *The Inner Light Magazine,* since published as *The Forgotten Mage,* edited by Dolores Ashcroft-Nowicki [Thoth Publications, 1999].

At this time Bernard Bromage also put at Dion Fortune's disposal material he had collected in his translation of Hindu tantrik texts, which led her to say that she had come to much the same conclusions as the Tantrists with regard to the interpenetration of the powers of mind and body.

As Bromage later wrote in his 1960 *Light* article on Dion Fortune,

"I recall many discussions with her on these and kindred topics: on the nature of the love technique and how it is the woman, the positive dynamism, who awakens the energy in the male and so makes him positive; of the part played by the ancestral subconscious in the formation of character and personality; of the tremendous and sometimes terrifying power of suggestion and its use in propaganda; of the nature of the child and the perception of animals. At this time I read all she had written and admired the courage and insight with which she probed the depths and stressed parallels which had not been sensed previously. A very active, ceaselessly speculative mind, with touches of genius."

Dion Fortune had always been interested in problems of human sexuality in society following her psychotherapeutic work at the Medico-Psychological Clinic from 1913 to 1916. As a direct result of this she had published, under her maiden name of Violet Firth, a little book based upon her counselling there called *The Problem of Purity* (1927), and as a consequence of her early esoteric work, *The Esoteric Philosophy of Love and Marriage* (1928), although both are arguably somewhat dated in light of subsequent social changes and attitudes. But stimulated by her discussions with Bernard Bromage a decade later, she wrote a more technical (and some thought dangerous!) work on the polar dynamics of the etheric vehicle, *The Circuit of Force.*[4] Like most of her work it first appeared as articles in *The Inner Light Magazine*, from February 1939 to August 1940, and eventually in volume form, supplemented by Gareth Knight, by Thoth Publications in 1998. It also expanded on her thoughts on the subject of ritual that she made in the course of various articles during the 1930s, since collected and published as *An Introduction to Ritual Magic* by Dion Fortune and Gareth Knight [Thoth Publications, 1997].

---

4 See Appendix 5 for an outline synopsis.

These works, in conjunction with *The Mystical Qabalah,* provide a complete theoretical backing to her novels. They reveal how, in her view, occultism is a study of little understood powers of the human mind and of the mind side of Nature. Therefore the first step in the pursuit of practical occultism is to train the mind, for only a very small proportion of occult work is concerned with phenomena perceived by the physical senses – it depends on the possession of some degree of psychic sensitivity for its appreciation. Yet psychism is really only hyper-sensitivity, and all of us are sensitive to a point, perhaps more so than we realise. We are receiving psychic impressions all the time, registering them subconsciously, and being influenced by them in varying degrees. Thus the whole of magical technique is a mental operation performed by the mind, and all the material paraphernalia of ceremonial and symbol are simply means to help the mind to concentrate and to exalt the imagination.

The deeper levels of the mind can be influenced by profound feeling and prolonged attention, and ritual is designed to take advantage of both methods. By means of a set rite we obtain prolonged attention, and by means of the "conditioned symbols" that make up the rite, we generate emotion. By means of a mood, or emotionally toned state of mind induced by the rite, we should be able to get in touch with a corresponding spiritual force. Thus by the use of that all-important factor, the pictorial imagination, the attention is held, a mood is achieved, and spiritual realisation or exaltation can follow.

The rules which govern the design of a ritual are the rules which govern the holding of attention. First and foremost is the emotionally charged idea and the symbol that represents it, whether it be a symbol to which we respond spontaneously or whether we have been "conditioned" to it. Then there is the appeal of sound through pitch and rhythm, an appeal which stirs the very foundations of our being. There is also the appeal of incense, which is a primordial appeal. Then there are the conditions under which a rite is performed, which should be such as to lull the mind and render it receptive. Therefore the effect of a ritual is most potent when it is performed in a dim light with all other sounds excluded so that there is nothing to distract the attention. Finally, there is the effect of reiteration, as is well known and exploited by the advertising industry.

There is, however, no aspect of occultism upon which more

foolishness is talked than upon ritual – the very mention of it is enough to crisp the hair! But ceremonial magic is simply mind power concentrated and co-ordinated by means of a formula. Although it is safe to say that if a spy were present at even the most exalted ceremonial, far from being blasted, it is only curiosity that would save the inquisitive individual from boredom.

Equally, on the other hand, it is folly to deny the power of ritual. But it is only powerful to affect the prepared mind, the mind of a person who has been "conditioned" to the symbols employed. It is obvious, therefore, that no casual observer will be even impressed, much less affected.

There is a kind of "subjective objectivity" in magical work, whereby images in consciousness take on power and become self-moving. We see this happen with compulsive ideas in psycho-pathology; but something of the same mechanism may be at work in certain magical phenomena (also in artistic creation), from which many practical applications open up.

The metaphysics of thought-forms is very complex but for all practical purposes the occultist acts "as if" they were objective, to induce the same feelings of awe and devotion and self-confidence as if they really were what they are presumed to be. The essence of the operation lies in the mind, and extraordinary things can be done with these thought-forms whether one can prove their objective existence or not.

Thus Dion Fortune believed that by utilising the subconscious element in our minds we are able to gain access to other planes of existence. As far as she was concerned, although the subconscious element was unquestionably important, it was hard to explain some of the experiences she had seen and heard on the assumption that it was subconsciousness and nothing more. Let us, then, she says, accept the subconscious, of whose ways we know a good deal, as our basis, but let us regard it as a means to an end and not an end in itself. Approaching the matter thus temperately, we are able to make a start and learn by experience.

It is in the plane of consciousness, the astro-mental plane, that results are experienced. It is the changing and energising of the mind whereby results are obtained. The mind thus energised becomes endowed with greatly extended powers, among which are clairvoyance, and telepathy of a type quite unrealised by the uninitiated, and the capacity to get into touch with cosmic forces which further reinforce its energies.

So by going to work "as if" these cosmic forces had objective existence and could exert influence, we obtain results; and it is noteworthy that the more confidence a person has in their objective existence, the better results are obtained. Although it should also be said that to believe in it superstitiously is to be haunted by bugaboos.

Yet by having faith in the coming of a "real presence", of whatever nature, power comes into the rite. Rationalise it away, and the ceremony will be inert. To understand that the power brought through by a thought-form can be an ensouling cosmic force, renders the work real and potent. This constitutes the technique of magic, and applies to whatever matter is at hand.

And it was with the intention of making some of these ideas available to a wider audience that Dion Fortune conceived the idea of writing novels containing practical instances of ritual at work – albeit with a certain amount of artistic licence as behoves the demands of a popular novel. And later to embark upon a series of publicly performed rituals – notably the Rite of Isis and the Rite of Pan – that had been back of the ideas in her novels.

The general outline of these novels was as follows, quoting largely from the (not wholly satisfactory) blurbs of recent editions, for they have been in and out of print by various publishers since their inception seventy years ago!

The Winged Bull

Brangwyn, an old wise magician, overhears an invocation to Pan outside the British Museum. Out of curiosity he answers the invoker and is surprised to find Murchison, an old acquaintance. With ritual matchmaking in mind, he offers Murchison employment. Brangwyn's sister has been caught up with a young occultist who has left her magically bonded to him and desperately unhappy – Murchison is to take part in a rite to free Ursula from this evil influence. He bravely infiltrates a Black Mass held by her captor in which she is to be the sacrificial victim in an obscene and dangerous ritual, a fate quite literally worse than death...

Actually no formal ritual is published in this novel. Dion Fortune was obviously just beginning to feel her way into this kind of project. However, basic ritual principles are described and the great god Pan is mentioned in passing in this book about twenty times even though no mention of a Rite of Pan is made.

The principle is contained in the alternative concept of a winged bull – which in some respects might be considered a considerably more potent image of masculine sexuality, as in Zeus and Europa. The immediate imagery is however based upon the Assyrian winged bulls that are displayed at the British Museum (although Dion Fortune erroneously refers to them as Babylonian) which are comparatively quite decorous and almost philosophical.

The esoteric connections in the ritual are concerned more with the polarity of Sun and Earth, and in the ritual sequence Ted Murchison appears as a Priest of the Sun and Ursula Brangwyn as a Priestess of the Earth. The ritual is a more or less a spontaneous one, using the power of music rather than words, and such words as there are, are quotations from Swinburne's poem *The Last Oracle*. There is also a sub-plot of black magicians trying to do their worst, which adds an element of adventure to the story, but little in terms of instructive practical magic except as an example perhaps of what *not* to do.

The Goat-Foot God

Desperate and wretched after the death of his wife at the hands of her lover, Hugh Paston becomes engrossed in the occult and goes on a quest for Pan, the goat-foot god, aided by an old bookseller called Jelkes. In order to fulfil his desire, the two buy an old monastery and convert it to a temple for Pan. The monastery, however, is haunted by the spirit of a 15th century prior, who was walled up in the cellar for his pagan beliefs and who is also searching for the goat-foot god. He intends to possess Paston and use his body as a vehicle to fulfil his own aims. But it all begins to go horribly wrong, with Jelkes' niece Mona holding the key to success or failure...

One or two short extracts from Rite of Pan appear in the book, although not in a ritual context. There are brief preliminaries leading up to a ritual in a bosky grove that is an ancient sacred site, but the actual rite and whatever else might have occurred after the final paragraph is left to the reader's imagination. The occasion also happens to be the couple's wedding night so, whatever may have happened, they retain a certain degree of respectability for the readers of 1930s romantic novels. Nonetheless the plot is well conceived esoterically, with interesting speculation between theories of haunting, reincarnation, and psychopathology all making their claims as to the working out of a problem which is eventually resolved by ritual means. There are no baddies providing ersatz conflict as in her previous fictional work.

The Sea Priestess

In The Sea Priestess, Dion Fortune introduces her most powerful and archetypal female character, the adept Vivien Le Fay Morgan. Morgan, a reincarnation of the Atlantean sea priestess who saved England from being submerged, meets the asthmatic Wilfred Maxwell who is in the throes of a midlife crisis. After literally enchanting Maxwell, the two start a series of magical workings. This culminates in a ritual and one of the most important magical lessons of the book where he assumes the role of a god, all men in one, to her goddess. Morgan eventually departs, leaving Maxwell to struggle with bringing the lesson learned in the practice of magic to the rest of his rather mundane life.

Almost the whole of the Rite of Isis is to be found in this book, albeit in fragmented form, along with the detailed preparation of a temple for it. Dion Fortune has obviously gained confidence in coming out with details of ritual even if it is not provided in a specific sequence. The sea priestess disappears somewhat melodramatically towards the end of the book but there remains an important sequel somewhat overlooked by the blurb writer, in that Wilfred Maxwell and his wife Molly set about living their lives according to magical principles, including a celebration of the rites as taught by the mysterious Vivien Le Fay Morgan.

Moon Magic

Moon Magic is the sequel to Dion Fortune's most acclaimed novel, The Sea Priestess. It continues the story of her hero, Vivien Le Fay Morgan, this time in the guise of Lilith Le Fay, setting up a temple dedicated to the worship of

Isis in London. There, through telepathic means, she attracts the service of the dour, repressed, yet psychically gifted Dr Rupert Malcolm as a participant in her magical workings — the priest to her priestess in their astral temple. During the course of her magical work, Le Fay breaks down Malcolm's querulous personality and helps him rediscover his emotional nature. At the apogee of their magical practice, he assumes the role of god to Le Fay's goddess as they combine their power in a supreme act of magic to benefit the whole human race.

Some parts of the Rite of Isis are included, although not quite so much as in the previous work. Although started in 1937 the novel was not completed by Dion Fortune, and it was finished (probably the last three chapters) by one of her close associates for publication in 1956. It provides some details of Lilith's temple in a converted church on the south bank of the Thames not unlike the Belfry in external appearance, although that was some way north of the river, in Belgravia.

The magical principles upon which the rites in the novels work is a triangular structure – Priest, Priestess, and High Priest. That is to say masculine and feminine polar dynamics overseen by a hierophantic figure. Thus Brangwyn oversees Ted and Ursula in *The Winged Bull*, Jelkes advises Hugh and Mona in *The Goat-Foot God*, and an inner plane Priest of the Moon – a kind of Merlin figure – is behind Vivien and Wilfred in *The Sea Priestess*, although less overtly in *Moon Magic*.

In terms of the interplay of characters in each novel, we are concerned with the redemption, so to speak, of a somewhat unbalanced hero, by magical polarisation with a woman through the technique of ritual, although the end result changes in the sequence of the novels. In *The Winged Bull* and *The Goat-Foot God* the denouement is the marriage of the couple, who in the first instance seem quite incompatible in almost every conceivable way. In *The Sea Priestess* and in *Moon Magic* any thought of such a conclusion is written off right from the start, the priestess is concerned with her own level of magical work and not with any physical or marital liaison. Although as a consequence of being used in this way, her trainee priest, after her departure, is left in a position to form a fruitful social and magical partnership of his own.

Beyond the personal level, as the sea priestess herself describes, the rites should help to lay down dynamics that may have some effect upon the soul of society at large, by operating on what psychologists might call the collective unconscious or occultists the astral light. All this in the context of some of the tightly buttoned up inhibitions of 1920s and 1930s society. And more directly, Dion Fortune hoped that the novels might have a releasing and initiatory effect upon any of her readers who associated themselves with one of the key characters.[5] Little did circulating library subscribers of the late 1930s realise what they might be letting themselves in for!

In the chapters that follow we shall take a more detailed look at the novels themselves in the context of the Rites of Pan and Isis written and performed by Dion Fortune and her colleagues at the time.

---

5 See her articles on the subject in Appendices 2 and 3.

2
RITUAL WORKING
IN THE WINGED BULL

THE ritual sequence in *The Winged Bull* is overseen by Colonel Brangwyn as High Priest or Hierophant, with the polar positions being taken by his half-sister Ursula Brangwyn and ex-army comrade Ted Murchison. The purpose of it is to bring about an emotional liaison between the two that will eventually lead to marriage.

It appears that this kind of ritual has been enacted before, between Ursula and Frank Fouldes, a former esoteric student of Brangwyn's, who has however badly fallen from grace in coming under the sway of Hugo Astley, a magician with a distinctly unsavoury reputation. Following this he has emotionally dominated Ursula by means of hypnosis, with the intention of using her in one of Astley's dubious rites – a Rite of the Bull rather than a Rite of the Winged Bull.

The purpose of the present use of the rite is to establish Ted Murchison in Ursula's affections in place of Frank Fouldes. This is not helped by the fact that Ted and Ursula have little in common, and are opposite types in a number of ways. Ted is Nordic, socially gauche and extraverted, whilst Ursula is Celtic, socially sophisticated and introverted. Added to which, unlike Ursula, Ted has no previous knowledge of occultism at all, and has to be taught from scratch.

This initial ignorance, and need to be trained, is a common theme in the other novels too – Hugh Paston in *The Goat-Foot God*, Wilfred Maxwell in *The Sea Priestess*, and Rupert Malcolm in *Moon Magic* – and enables Dion Fortune to incorporate basic occult teaching into her novels for the benefit of readers who may well be similarly uninstructed in these matters.

However, the opposing aspects of Ted and Ursula – in background and in character – are put to good use, for as Dion Fortune explains in her article analysing this book,[6] their personal differences reflect a similar condition in the soul of the nation. Thus a reconciliation of any differences between Ursula and Ted can form a talismanic reconciliation of deep divisions within the nation, that for instance go back in legendary terms to the battle of the Red Dragon against the White that undermined Vortigern's castle in the vision of Merlin, the red dragon of Wales against the white of the Saxons, the Wars of the Roses – the red of Lancaster against the white of York, and so on.

The ritual is fairly simple and largely spontaneous, enacted by dance, to the evocative music of the High Priest's violin. Broadly speaking it involves Murchison identifying himself with the Sun and Ursula with the Earth, in keeping with the poetic quotation to be found at the beginning of the book by the poet William Watson.

> *For of old the Sun, our sire,*
> *came wooing the mother of men,*
> *Earth, that was virginal then,*
> *vestal fire to his fire.*
> *Silent her bosom and coy,*
> *but the strong god sued and pressed;*
> *and born of their starry nuptial joy*
> *are all that drink of her breast.*

In keeping with his solar priestly function Murchison is robed in nothing but a straight-hanging, sleeveless garment of heavy gold tissue, cut on the lines of that of an ancient Egyptian priest, a rayed golden sun disk embroidered on the breast. Gold sandals and a golden fillet about his fair hair like a sun-god's halo all round it, a broad band round the hips, like the sash on a priest's cassock, complete his outfit.

Ursula, for her part, is clad in a filmy, flowing green robe that billows round her like a cloud, hanging from a narrow band of gold about her breast, and flowing as she moves "like wind-blown smoke".

6　See Appendix 3.

A gold fillet binds her dark hair that hangs free – she also wears gold sandals on her bare feet.

On entering the temple each assumes the posture of an ancient Egyptian god, sitting bolt upright, knees and feet together, hands along thighs. In his prior instruction to the couple Brangwyn has told them that when they have entered the temple and taken their seats:

> *"I shall chant, and invoke, and play my violin. When the spirit moves you, you start to perform your parts. You take the initiative, Murchison, at least, I expect you will. Now bear this in mind, and picture it in your imagination — Ursula represents the earth in spring. You are the sun-god gathering strength as the days lengthen. My music and my chanting, if I do my part properly, ought to cause images to rise in your imagination; accept these images as if they were real, and live in your imagination as the rite goes on. That is the aim of it — to stir the imagination. This is a kind of psychology the schools know nothing about. You will know something about it, though, before you have finished, and you will see how extraordinarily effectual it is. When you really get into it, and feel as if it were real, but not before — don't budge before it becomes real to you, Murchison, or it will be a fiasco, and worse than useless — act out the play as you feel it. I don't know what will come to you, and I shall be very interested to see."*

The temple wherein they are to perform is a spacious soundproof basement lit by half a dozen candles in high ecclesiastical candlesticks ranged in a circle round the room. Walls, floor and ceiling and every article of temple furniture are painted a shining gold, reflecting the candle light back again and again so that the very air seems to glow with golden light. They take their seats on throne-like chairs of gilded wood, one on each side of the room. Towards the far end of the room is a small square altar, a little over three foot square, also of bright gold, on which stands a rough pitcher of unglazed earthenware with a mass of pine branches in it, the resinous needles smelling aromatically in the warmth of the room. Around the pitcher are a cup of curious shape three parts full of very dark wine, a platter of broken bread, and a small dish of coarse salt. The shape of the cup is similar to the one famously said to have been moulded by an ancient king from the breast of Helen of Troy. The altar and the seats of Ursula and Ted form an equilateral triangle.

The fourth side of the room, the one by which they entered, has a raised curtained platform, reached by three steps, which conceals the entrance door so that the dais can be entered without being observed by anyone already in the temple. Upon his entry Brangwyn thus mounts the dais unobserved, and from behind the concealing curtain sounds a single note from a bell, before chanting the traditional warning cry of the Dionysiac Mysteries *"Hekas, Hekas, este bibeloi!"* – that is to say *"Begone ye profane ones!"* bidding the uninitiated to flee from the path of the divinely inebriated revellers lest they be torn to pieces by them.

Then the violin begins to play, first suggesting running water or the wind in the trees, then deepening and strengthening to evoke the thought of summer woods in deep leaf and full of bird song, to pass on to a rushing, circling fire music like the sun's corona of towering flames. Then, after this wordless evocation of Earth and Sun, the curtains on the dais part, and Brangwyn appears at the top of the three steps, in a great golden cope shot with salmon pink, and on his head the headdress of united crowns of Upper and Lower Egypt with the Uraeus-serpent reared before it. Stretching out his hands to indicate that the others stand, in a sonorous voice he begins to intone the words of the poet Swinburne, which is an invocation to the Sun god.

> *Years have risen and fallen in darkness or in twilight,*
> *ages waxed and waned that knew not thee or thine,*
> *while the world sought light by night and sought not thy light,*
> *since the last sad pilgrim left thy dark mid-shrine.*
> *Dark the shrine and dumb the fount of song thence welling,*
> *save for words more sad than tears of blood, that said;*
> *"Tell the king, on earth has fallen the glorious dwelling,*
> *and the water-springs that spake are quenched and dead."*
>
> *And he bowed down his hopeless head*
> *in the drift of the wild world's tide.*
> *And dying, "Thou hast conquered," he said,*
> *"Galilean"; he said it, and died.*
>
> *Yea, not yet we see thee, father, as they saw thee,*
> *they that worshipped when the world was theirs and thine,*

*they whose words had power by thine own power to draw thee
down from heaven till earth seemed more than heaven divine.*

*To the likeness of one God their dreams enthralled thee,
who wast greater than all gods that waned and grew;
Son of God the shining Son of Time they called Thee,
who wast older, O our father, than they knew.*

*Old and younger gods are buried and forgotten
from uprising to downsetting of thy sun,
risen from eastward, fallen to westward and forgotten,
and their births are many, but their end is one.
Diverse births of godheads find one death appointed,
as the soul whence each was born makes room for each;
god by god goes out, discrowned and disanointed,
but the soul stands fast that gave them life and speech.*

*Day by day Thy shadow shines in heaven beholden,
even the sun, the shining shadow of Thy face;
King, the ways of heaven before Thy feet grow golden;
God, the soul of heaven is kindled with Thy grace.*

*As they knew Thy name of old time could we know it,
healer called of sickness, slayer invoked of wrong,
light of eyes that saw Thy light, God, king, priest, poet,
song should bring Thee back to heal us with Thy song.*

*For Thy Kingdom is passed not away,
nor Thy power from the place therefore hurled;
out of heaven they shall cast not the day,
they shall cast not out song from the world.*

*By the song and the light they give
we know Thy works that they live;
with the gift Thou hast given us of speech
we praise, we adore, we beseech,
we arise at Thy bidding and follow,
we cry to Thee, answer, appear,*

O Father of all of us, Paian, Apollo,
destroyer and healer, hear!

The curtains of the dais fall back into place, and from behind them the music begins again, wild music, gypsy music, syncopated rhythms from Africa. Murchison feels that the music is being used to whip him up to some tremendous change of consciousness – he begins to breathe deeply and rhythmically in time to the music, and as he does, feels a kind of tide beginning to flow in and out of him, waxing and waning with the curious pulsating rhythm. Then with no break into its sequence the music slides into the tremendous pealing of the chant:

O all ye works of the Lord, bless ye the Lord: praise Him and magnify Him
for ever!
Sun, moon and stars bless ye the Lord: praise Him and magnify Him for
ever!

The room becomes quiet, with a stillness like extreme pressure, as if something is about to burst, then there comes a slow limpid rhythmless tune, not unlike a Gregorian chant, exceedingly archaic, and Murchison feels a curious glow of warmth and something behind him, overshadowing him, as if with a pair of hawk's wings. He feels a sudden deep trilling in his throat and then a voice such as he has never heard before burst out from him; *"Ra! Ra! Ra!"*

There follows a dead silence, as he has enough wits left to realise that this is mediumship he is experiencing – with a god for control! A curious sense of helplessness comes over him and a slight fear, before he feels the humming gather strength in his throat again, to break forth with:

"I am Horus, god of the morning; I mount the sky on eagle's wings.
I am Ra in mid-heaven; I am the sun in splendour. I am Toum of the
downsetting. I am Kephra at midnight. Thus spake the priest with the
mask of Osiris."

…which is the cue for Brangwyn, the High Priest upon the dais, to respond, his hands raised in invocation:

"Helios! Helios! Helios!"

Now Murchison finds himself back in waking consciousness, but with a difference, as everything that was Ted Murchison has been swept away and he is in some deep primeval level of consciousness – in the Oldest Land – of a forgotten race – and he has Knowledge. He is about to play his part in a great sun rite to bring life and fertility to the earth and inspiration to the heart of man. He rises from his seat and takes three steps towards the earth priestess opposite, who rises and takes three steps towards him, and so the rite begins.

He has no very clear remembrance of the rite, either at that time or afterwards, but he recalls that they seemed to be dancing together, in the course of which they came up to the altar and drank together from the cup of dark resinous-tasting wine, ate together of the broken bread dipped in the coarse salt, and inhaled the fragrance of the pine-branches with their little dark cones.

Which was all there was to it on the physical plane, but inwardly there was much more going on. They were not two individual persons but two forces. He the sun in heaven bringing life to the earth; she the earth absorbing it hungrily, drawing it from him to satisfy her crying needs, and the more she drew from him the more flowed into him. He felt himself all brightness, as if he were compact of shining gold, and he felt the woman in his arms gradually light up like the earth at dawn as the sun steals over the line of the eastern hills, until finally she too was all brightness, and they were made as one, as they slowly circled to the slow three fold rhythm of the music, until finally, the music moving ever more slowly to a silence, they stand before the altar, hands of blessing extended over them by the High Priest, as consciousness came back to normal.

It should be said that this level of experience is hardly likely to be met with in real life, particularly at a first attempt! But that for the purposes of the novel, events have to be speeded up somewhat. And a beginner's reactions are more likely to be as Dion Fortune describes Ted Murchison's first reactions on entering the temple. Then he found a certain swinging between inner and outer consciousness, as at first he simply observed what was around him physically. It gave him an opportunity to regard Ursula at length as she sat opposite him, her eyes closed. She had a certain beauty about her that he found attractive, calling to his mind an image of the lover of a hero, Lady Hamilton, the mistress of Lord Nelson. This gives way to consideration of the aloof fastidiousness written in every line of her body and he experiences a feeling of rejection, then of pity for the man who might marry her, leading to a sudden dislike for her, as something male within him resents her atmosphere of virginal untouchability.

Then with a sudden surge of satiric mirth and mischief he wonders what it would be like to knock her off her pedestal and roll her in the earth. For a moment he identifies with the figure of a goat god chasing a nymph, then pulls himself together as he recalls who he is, and in the company of his employer and his employer's sister. Immediately the glamour of the temple furnishings fall away from his gaze and he sees them merely as painted plywood and curtains bought from drapery stores, the golden thrones as gilded chairs from some cheap antique shop.

This mood as quickly passes as he looks at Ursula again, thinking she looks tense and apprehensive, and the goat mood gives way to a feeling of sympathy for a fellow human being.

These are the typical feelings of a personality of the outer world. But as the rite begins and the lines from *The Last Oracle* are being chanted he begins to experience a different mode of consciousness. To feel the desolation of a world deserted by its god. To feel the misery and frustrations of the world flowing over him. As he begins to feel an actual part of it, rather than reacting to it with a personal depression as the chanting tells of a dying god.

Following from this come to mind thoughts of the great Roman emperor Julian the Apostate, as a note of furtive triumph creeps into the words, as if an awakening of the old gods is at hand to break through the repressions of medieval piety. Who is this unnamed god who is being invoked, he asks himself, whose power that he feels is beginning to fill the room?

Then there flickers before his inward vision a landscape like the surface of the moon, and in the centre of it, Saturn, the oldest of the Olympian gods. And there comes a moment of revelation as he suddenly realises the faith for which he has been searching, in the one great Creator and Sustainer of the Universe, whose form changes with the increase in the powers of mankind's understanding. The real Being behind all gods. A God who is so many-sided that no one can see every side at once. There is a Christian facet, an Old Testament facet, a Hindu facet, a Taoist facet, many pagan facets – a God as many-sided as the soul and the faiths of man.

After the ritual Brangwyn starts a discussion with Murchison about what it might have been all about, and opens up with the statement *"You see how we use ritual to work up a particular emotional state, and while you are in that state how something magnetic flows between you and Ursula"* and goes on to say *"Well, yesterday was just a trial run, but it showed you the possibilities, and that if you were trained as Ursula has been trained, there could be a great deal more in it that there was last night."*

"There was as much in it as I knew what to do with," Murchison replies, and asks *"What was it that spoke through me at one point in the proceedings?"* to be met with the somewhat ambivalent response:

"Ah, what indeed? If we knew that we should know a good deal. We don't know what these things are. At least I don't, though there are some people who think they do. We don't know what they are, we only know they are immensely powerful. It might be your subconscious; it might be telepathic suggestion from Ursula and me, for we were visualising for all we were worth. Or it might be what it purported to be, though I think myself that that is unlikely. My belief is that it is a mixture of all these. A great natural force, dramatised by your subconscious mind, just as Freud says repressed emotion is dramatised by dreams. It's only one remove from dreams to hallucinations, wherein a lunatic objectifies them and acts them out. These things are all first cousins to each other. If we knew all about one of them, we'd be able to explain the lot. But, as it is, we only know a little about all of them, and can explain nothing. But although we can't explain it, we can use it. We can't explain electricity, but we know how it is generated, and how conducted, and how to put it to work for heating, lighting and power. That temple is a generating station; the ritual, the dynamo; your imagination, the electric motor at the other end of the circuit; your larynx, the wheels of the tram that are turned by the motor. That's the best description I can give you. I can tell you what this thing does, but I cannot tell you what it is. By their fruits ye shall know them. Are not the fruits fullness of life? The gods are lenses that wise men have made through which to focus the great natural forces."

To Murchison's question as to what are these forces made out of, he replies *"Thought-stuff, my lad, thought-stuff. Are you any the wiser?"* and goes on to quote a little more Swinburne by way of a possible explanation.

For no thought of man made Gods to love and honour
ere the song within the silent soul began,
nor might earth in dream or deed take heaven upon her
till the word was clothed with speech by lips of man.

That is to say, that Swinburne thought that the old gods were not without significance, and that we lose a lot by neglecting them – principally the subconscious mind. So if we wake up the old gods again we recover the use of the subconscious mind and get in touch with great natural forces from which civilisation has cut us off.

Indeed the whole occult field in general had been recently equated with the Collective Unconscious of Jungian psychology. Brangwyn's attitude to Christianity reflects Dion Fortune's syncretic position, who was ready to embrace all faiths, regarding them as separate strands of one multiplex religious field. *"In my Father's house are many mansions."* Or as one sceptical critic called it, not without some truth "Anglicanism gone polytheistic".

A useful insight into Dion Fortune's approach is provided in a little invocation she wrote for the consecration of her sanctuary at Chalice Orchard, Glastonbury in 1932.

"Let us adore the Ancient Ones that we may be known of them and They may bless us in the sowing, in the reaping and in the baking; in the hearth fire, in the rooftree and in the byre, in the bed and at board; in the fighting and in the feasting. For Adonai is the Lord of the Kingdom of Earth. All things earthly are holy unto Him and the Gods of old time are His Voices. Blessed are those mighty Ones who speak with the Voice of Adonai; may we hear them with the inner ear and see them with the inner eye, and be blessed of Them in all that we do in the Kingdom of Nature."

As part of his esoteric training Murchison is enjoined to study psychology and to meditate on aspects of mythology, with emphasis on the technique known as the composition of place.

"It is the way Ignatius Loyola trained his Jesuits," Brangwyn explains, *"Only we apply it to other ends. The Jesuits visualise New Testament scenes and work up an extraordinary religious pressure. We visualise the old myths and work up pressures of quite a different kind."* As for instance that he had been working the "winged bull formula" with Ursula, and goes on

to explain: *"All these animal gods are psychological formulae just as H_2O is a chemical formula. In the old myths the bull is always a phallic symbol, meaning crude sexual force. The eagle's wings are spiritual aspiration — the flight to the sun. The human head is human intelligence. Put the three together, and how does the formula read? The powerful bull-form of the natural instincts soaring on eagle's wings of spiritual aspirations, with consciousness poised between them."*

"Do you understand the symbolism?" he asks Murchison.

"Not altogether," replies Murchison.

"You will if you don't let me down!"

And in the course of the book, despite many ups and downs, Murchison does not let either Colonel or Ursula Brangwyn down and all comes to a happy ending, which comes to pass in their marriage, as with Hugh Paston and Mona Freeman at the conclusion of *The Goat-Foot God* and Wilfred Maxwell and Molly Coke in *The Sea Priestess*. Not that all magical working ends in wedding bells but we are here still operating within the conventions of the romantic novel.

THE GOAT-FOOT GOD
& THE RITE OF PAN

ION Fortune's *Rite of Pan* must have been written, at least in part, during or before the time she was writing her novel *The Goat-Foot God*, for there are two sequences from it in the book. The first appears immediately before the first chapter, and is cited as being from *The Rite of Pan*.

Came the voice of Destiny,
calling o'er the Ionian Sea,
"The Great God Pan is dead, is dead.
Humbled is the hornèd head;
shut the door that hath no key —
waste the vales of Arcady."

Shackled by the Iron Age,
lost the woodland heritage,
heavy goes the heart of man,
parted from the light-foot Pan;
wearily he wears the chain
till the Goat-god comes again.

Half a man and half a beast,
Pan is greatest, Pan is least.
Pan is all, and all is Pan;

Look for him in every-man;
goat-hoof swift and shaggy thigh —
follow him to Arcady.

He shall wake the living dead —
cloven hoof and horned head,
human heart and human brain,
Pan the goat-god comes again!
Half a beast and half a man —
Pan is all, and all is Pan.

Come, O Goat-god, come again!

And the following, as a little song is sung by Mona Freeman as she dresses the breakfast table the morning after she had spontaneously danced her "moon dance" for the drawing out of Hugh Paston's soul from its monkish preoccupations.

Bowl of oak and earthen jar,
honey of the honey-bee;
milk of kine and Grecian wine,
golden corn from neighbouring lea —
these our offerings, Pan, to thee,
Goat-foot god of Arcady.

Hornèd head and cloven hoof —
fawns who seek and nymphs that flee —
piping clear and draweth near
through the vales of Arcady —
these the gifts we have of thee,
God of joyous ecstasy.

Come, great Pan, and bless us all:
bless the corn and honey-bee.
Bless the kine and bless the vine,
bless the vales of Arcady.
Bless the nymphs that laugh and flee,
God of all fertility.

Mona provides the feminine pole in the familiar triangular magical set up of a Dion Fortune novel, the male side being provided by Hugh Paston, a wealthy socialite whose world has fallen apart after having been betrayed by his wife and his best friend. As the couple were killed in a car crash he is a free agent matrimonially, but in his reaction against society, is flirting with the idea of taking up some kind of occultism of a possibly shady kind. He seeks the advice of an old antiquarian bookseller, Jelkes, who having once been a postulant to the Jesuit order before realising that the priesthood was not for him, is able to guide Hugh away from an unhealthy interest in 19th century French novels glamorising black magic, towards an interest in the classical pagan forms of worship, notably of Pan.

Jelkes thus provides the high priest figure in the magical action, although not in so direct a manner as Brangwyn in *The Winged Bull* or the Priest of the Moon in *The Sea Priestess*. Jelkes' role is more in the nature of an advisor, sometimes against his better judgment, as the wealthy Hugh decides to buy an old monastery building to practice some kind of pagan magic therein. Mona is Jelkes' adopted niece, a financially struggling freelance designer, who is taken on to help Hugh in the practicalities of refurbishing the old buildings of Monks Farm.

Needless to say, she is soon involved in the psychological restructuring of Hugh Paston as well, who upon taking up residence in the place, discovers that in the past it had been a kind of penal colony for a disgraced abbot, Brother Ambrosius, who had been attracted to the worship of Pan. As a consequence of this he and his monks were punished by being walled up in the place, the ecclesiastical authorities regarding the Great God Pan as synonymous with the Devil.

This provides the scenario for Hugh to find himself in a difficult bind, along with an intriguing puzzle for the reader, for we are never quite sure whether Ambrosius still haunts the place, and if he does, whether he is a former incarnation of Hugh Paston, who finds himself becoming obsessed with this monkish figure. Or is it simply a matter of psychopathology on the part of the somewhat unstable anti-hero, who also is half-inclined to regard Mona as a reincarnated female companion in ancient Greece, or even an elemental succubus dreamed up by the ancient monk.

In this mare's nest of possibilities Jelkes is somewhat stretched in his efforts to keep events upon an even track. Things work themselves out however by their investigations into the worship of Pan, in the course of which, helped by Mona, Hugh comes to terms with the Ambrosius figure, after which the place seems no longer haunted, and all seems likely to come to a happy ending, as Hugh and Mona get married and repair to the woods to celebrate the rites of Pan. On the way to this conclusion however, we are provided with some of Hugh's realisations as he comes to terms with things and learns the possibilities of magic.

Much of this is in terms of his conversations with Jelkes. As he remarks on one occasion:

> *"One expects psychic phenomena to be reasonably tangible and to have something of the miraculous about them. We've had nothing of that.... Nothing you could call evidential if you'd got any notion of the nature of evidence. But all the same we've had some pretty drastic experiences. I couldn't prove them to anybody else, and I'm not such a fool as to try to; but I'm quite satisfied about them in my own mind. Anyway, whatever they are, subconscious, super-conscious, hallucinations, telepathy, suggestion, auto-suggestion, cosmic experiences, bunk, spoof or hokum, I feel as if I had been born again. Not saved. Or ever likely to be. Or ever likely to want to be. But born into a wider life and a bigger personality. That's good enough for me.*
>
> *"How do I know it isn't all your imagination? I don't know and don't care. It probably is, for I've used my imagination diligently enough over the job. But* **via** *the imagination I've got extended consciousness, which I probably should never have been able to make a start on if I'd stuck to hard facts all along and rejected everything I couldn't prove at the first go.*
>
> *"It's no use doing that. You've got to take the Unseen as a working hypothesis, and then things you can't prove at the first go prove themselves later.*
>
> *"By going ahead 'as if' it were true, I've got in touch with another kind of reality — and in that kind of reality I can pull strings that make things happen.*
>
> *"But you've got to handle it along its own lines. That's the mistake people make — expecting miracles. Thinking if they say the word of power things will happen. But they won't unless you've worked up the power of the word first of all. Old Ignatius was right, if it was him who said — 'Live the life and you'll develop the faith'. I want to invoke Pan."*

To Jelkes, Pan is seen as very much in terms of a general opener to the subconscious, to the racial memory, to the biological memory, or the morphological memory – because he stands for lack of repression. From this the way can lead to any of the more specialised gods such as those of Mount Olympus. In a final summing up of where they are at, he recommends reading Jung's *The Secret of the Golden Flower*, together with Coué on induced autosuggestion, Iamblichos on the bringing of power to the Egyptian gods by the force of imagination, and St Ignatius on the visualisation training of the Jesuits.

And in conversation with Mona, Hugh asks her about the attitude of Jelkes to religion and to magic, who replies:

"Did you know he once studied for the priesthood?"

"Yes, he told me. And he's still a priest at heart. You can see that. Tell me, is he a Christian or a pagan? I can't make him out."

"He's a Christian at heart, but he won't stand for the narrowness of Christian theology."

"What is there in Christianity beyond the theology?"

"Why, there's just as much power as there is in Pan, only of a different kind."

"Would you call yourself a Christian?"

"No, I shouldn't. But I'm not anti-Christian. I see it as one of the Paths."

"Paths to what?"

"Paths to the Light."

"You wouldn't get a Christian to admit there was more than one Path."

"I know. And that's the pity of it. That's what spoils Christianity. It's too limited."

"What does Uncle Jelkes say about your pagan proclivities."

"It was he who put me on to them. I had a terribly strict upbringing and it disagreed with me most actively. Father thought an art school was an abode of sin. Then I met Uncle Jelkes, and he made me understand a lot of things I'd never understood before. My natural self said: 'You'll have to give up Christianity. It's disagreed with you. It isn't for everybody.' And he put me on to the old Greek gods, and I simply loved them. My headaches got better and my drawing improved out of sight. He says, and I'm certain he's right, that there is a tremendous lot in the old Greek gods. There are great truths there that we have forgotten."

"Does he propose to scrap Christianity?"

"Oh no. But he thinks the Greek viewpoint is a very valuable corrective to it."

"It certainly needs something done to it," says Hugh.

"It does indeed. It is not meeting the need of the world as it is at present. And it isn't just the worldly people who are leaving it. Nor the sceptical. It is people like Uncle Jelkes and you and me, who want more of God than they can find in it."

"What kind of God do you want that you can't find in it?"

"I want God made manifest in Nature — that's Pan you know."

Mona goes forward with Hugh's intentions on the strength of a feeling of dedication to all that is natural and true and good. In a rather striking image she sees Pan as a leader of the goats, as opposed to the church which she feels is a leader of the sheep. She imagines Pan as a kind of underworld Apollo, holding out a crook to lead the creatures of the flock of Ishmael, the misfits who find no place in the world of towns and men – the keep of all wild and hunted souls. Thus the real invocation of Pan is a surrender to the bed rock of natural fact rather than a striving after an unreal spirituality. Whereas St Francis spoke of the body as Brother Ass she sees man as a centaur, akin to the winged horse, Pegasus – where we have a resonance with the imagery of *The Winged Bull*. Mona feels reassured, come what may, and feels that she has the blessing of Pan.

This combination of Biblical and pagan imagery is typical of Dion Fortune, and her sympathy with the latter is one facet of her having become something of an icon for the modern neo-pagan movement despite her, albeit unorthodox, Christian affiliations.

And in pursuit of the worship of Pan, Hugh finds the way ahead in a number of waking visions.

Thus as he stands on the site of the old abbey building, the bare grey stones seem to give place to the white marble of a Greek temple, and the pale starlight to flickering Greek torches. He is the priest in the sanctuary awaiting the coming of the priestess. Beyond the curtains, Tyrian-dyed, he can hear the murmur of an excited crowd in the temple. The curtains part, and the priestess of Ceres, in the form of Mona, stands before him, the curtains falling behind her. The crowded temple is hushed and holds its breath. This is the sacrament, the bringing through of power, the sacerdotal office. Behind him is the All-Father, the First-Begotten Love, behind her is the Earth-Mother. As in his fantasy that he had become the priest, he now spontaneously becomes the god. He feels the power come over him and realises himself part of a larger whole, made one with the earth as she swings through the circling heavens.

Then he is suddenly checked and stayed. He can go no further. He lacks his priestess. The power that sought expression through him can find no passage, for the circuit does not lead to earth but remains insulated in empty space. The reaction hits him hard. He knows that he has been within an ace of the thing he sought, but the incident leaves him with no more than a sense of irritated frustration.

On a later occasion his mind turns back to Arcady, where alone lies the fulfilment of both promise and dream. The Arcadian Pan with his shepherd's pipe is no diabolical deity, like the sinister Goat of Mendes of the inflamed medieval imagination. It is the thing that Ambrosius must have gone after – the Greek inspiration that had awakened him to his manhood. He reflects on the curious fact that when men began to re-assemble the fragments of Greek culture, a Renaissance came to a medieval civilisation that had sat in intellectual darkness since the days when the gods had withdrawn. What was going to happen in our own day, now that Freud had come along crying: "Great Pan is risen!" – ?

He wonders whether his own problems are not part of a universal problem, and his own awakening part of a much wider awakening? He wonders how far the realisation of an idea by one man, even if he spoke no word, might inject into the group-mind of the race and set it working like a ferment?

Supposing, he thinks, he were to fantasise the part of a Greek high-priest until it became alive in him. Might not Mona answer to it? For some reason best known to herself she had made open confession when they had been psychoanalysing themselves in the chapel. Why had she done that? Was there something in Mona that was saying, *"Yes, I will worship Pan with you provided you are of the true faith?"*

It seems to him that if he could pull this thing off with Mona – this curious experience of time as a mode of consciousness, and this even more curious experiment in the power of the day-dream – something would be brought through into the group-mind of the race and added to the racial heritage. He has no need to appeal to his fellow-men or seek their suffrage and support; he has only got to *be* something – *do* something, and the thing would start in the group-soul of the race which would feel it subconsciously. That, at any rate, was the way Jelkes said the adepts worked.

It comes to him again as he stares at the marvel of the night-sky – realising that he is part of a greater whole, and that a vast life finds expression through him. That in *his* fulfilment *it* would find a measure of *its* fulfilment. That in *his* frustration *it* was frustrated. It was not a question of Hugh Paston being in love with a woman who did not respond to him. It was a question of unbalanced force in the universe. And the whole universe was striving to adjust that unbalance. So if he could but lean back and let himself be borne by the cosmic tides, they should bring him to the place where he ought to be. But to achieve that, he must lean back, and let go. Allow the cosmic forces to adjust themselves in their own way. For not otherwise could he take advantage of them.

He feels he has stumbled on a very important key when he realises that the way of approach to the dynamic reality might be the path of fantasy – the most dynamic of all forms of auto-suggestion. It might be pure imagination, but nevertheless it was the way to set the invisible causes in motion, provided it lay along the line of their course.

This was indeed a discovery worth making. He had only to become the priest and he could command his priestess. Not that it was a case of dominating Mona; it was a case of himself becoming the thing that would answer to the need in her. She knew too much to be content with a commonplace mating; what she wanted was the priest-initiator. If he could make himself this, she would marry him all right, no need to worry about that. It was not Mona that was his problem, but *he* that was Mona's problem.

But how was he to do this thing? How was he to ordain himself to the priesthood of a forgotten rite? How save by letting the power of which it was the expression rise up with its own peculiar magnetism, so that deep called unto deep?

As far as the book is concerned, this begins and ends with the invocation and the rite of Pan.

For the Rite of Pan Hugh has the good fortune to find an old sacred site. Within a little wood of Scotch firs is a close belt of ancient yew trees that form a narrow oval-shaped glade in the form of a *vesica piscis* (the shape that is formed by two interconnecting circles). And in the centre of this is a fallen megalith, which locals refer to as one of the "Devil's Skittles" and best not moved. However, restoring it to an upright position seems harmless enough. On close examination it is certainly a worked stone, of a rock different from the local chalk, and in the form of a short blunt pillar with a rounded top (i.e. phallic). There is a herb walk on the way to it, at the end of which are two grey bushes, known as goat-herbs on account of the smell of goat that they give off if brushed against.

The full moon rides high in a cloudless sky on the night of their wedding day at the local church, and Venus, the evening star, is visible just over the pines as the couple make their way to the site. Mona is dressed in floating green from which the moonlight takes all the colour, so that she looks like a grey wraith. Hugh himself wears the traditional fawn skin.

They go down between the herb borders, hoary silver in the dusk, and into the pine woods through an arch cut in the belt of yews, to come out into the little lozenge shaped glade bathed in moonlight. Dozens of rabbits scurry away, all except one baby thing that takes refuge in the shadow of the pillar and stays throughout the proceedings, as if representing its Master, the Lord of the Wild.

Hugh, offering no explanation, places Mona at one end of the enclosure and takes up his own position at the other, and waits for inspiration as he has no idea what a rite of Pan might be. His thoughts go back to his dream of the hills of Greece, and he follows in his mind the path of the dreams, up the steep hillside, through the sparse wood, and then, almost involuntarily the deeper wood where he feels the cold pang of fear that lurks there waiting for him. He feels it in his solar plexus, like a hand gripping, and shudder goes all over him. He sees the hanging points of Mona's drapery flutter and knows that she has shuddered too. Then he sees between them a path of pale gold light that is not moonlight.

A breath of wind begins to stir in the narrow space between the encircling yews, a little cold breath of air that moves softly over them, as if feeling them, pauses, and moves on again and is gone. Then the temperature starts to rise, steadily and rapidly. Hugh feels the sweat break out on his chest, left bare by the fawn skin, and finds it hard to breathe, his breath coming short and quick. The band of light across the turf rises hip high and binds him to Mona as the current binds a man to the live rail. It is far stronger than he expected and again comes the pang of fear.

Then the place begins to fill with light, overpowering the oppressive heat so that they forget the heat and think only of light. It is a curious light, neither of the sun, nor of the moon, nor of the stars; more silvery than the golden band that still shines amid it; less silvery than the pale moon-glow and the stars. And in this light all things are reflected. The earth spreads away into space in a great curve, with their grove upon it. It swings through the heavens in a yet greater curve, the planets circling round it, and is ringed, like Saturn, with luminous bands. This is the earth aura, and within it their life is lived. Their psychic selves breathe in the atmosphere. And within the earth is the earth-soul, all alive and sentient, from which they draw their vitality.

Mona knew that these things are there all the time, though in their normal state they were unaware of them; but Hugh thinks they have come at his invocation, and feels that the whole swinging sphere circles about him, and for a brief moment knows godhead.

The glade is softly luminous, very hot, as a band of glowing gold, like illuminated smoke, stretches from Hugh to Mona, flowing around the pillar, whose conical top rises just above it. Behind Hugh is the newly-risen moon so his face is in darkness, but Mona's face shows clear in the moonlight. He can see her eyes, but she cannot see his, and her look has a blankness in consequence, as if she were looking beyond him at something that stands behind him. Perhaps she was, for at that moment a gradually dawning awareness makes itself felt, and Hugh knows that something is behind him, vast and overshadowing, and from it emanates the band of light that passes through him to fall on Mona. He feels himself getting vaster and vaster, and about to burst with the force that is upon him. He is towering up, his head among the stars; below him, Mona and the earth lie in darkness. But over the earth-bend the advancing line of dawn is creeping up. Dimly he wonders if they had been in the grove all night, unconscious of the passage of time; then he realises that this is no earthly dawn, but the coming of the sun-god.

It is not the goat-god, crude and earthy. It is the sun! But not the sun of the sophisticated Apollo, but an older, earlier, primordial sun, the sun of Helios the Titan.

Hugh had not known what Freudian deeps they would work through in the name of the goat-god, and was prepared for anything, but this golden exaltation of high space takes him completely by surprise. Then he remembers the favourite phrase of old Jelkes: *"All the gods are one god, and all the goddesses are one goddess, and there is one initiator."* The All-Father was celestial Zeus – *and* woodland Pan – *and* Helios the Life-giver. He was all these things, and having known Pan, a man might pass on to the heavenly gate where Helios waits beside the Dawn.

Hugh feels his feet winged with fire, and knows that he is coming as the Angel of the Annunciation came to the Virgin; he is coming as the messenger of the Life-giver. Far below him Mona waits in the earth-shadow, and it seems to him that she is in some way lying back upon the earth and sunk in it, like a swimmer floating in water. He knows he is coming swiftly on the wings of the dawn, coming up with the dawn-wind as it circles the earth. He can see the line of golden light advance, and knows that his return to the grove will coincide with its coming.

Then he finds himself standing in the grove, in his own body, clad in the fawn-skin, with the line of light just beyond his feet. For the first time since the vision began he moves, taking a step forward. The line of light advances with him. He takes another step forward; it advances again. Mona has also taken two paces forward. He moves again, and the light and the woman move also.

Now as they stand face to face upon either side of the pillar, Hugh raises his bare arms and stretches them over Mona's head, and the light that had enveloped him spreads over her also. Then, raising his right hand in the Salute of the Sun as the Roman legions raised it, he lowers the left, tingling and burning with a strange heat, lays the flat palm between Mona's breasts and cries the ancient cry –

"Hekas, Hekas, este bibeloi! Be far from us, O ye profane!"

There the book ends, and we may presume that – however unlikely the scenario in the circumstances – they would have proceeded spontaneously to enact a rite such as that which follows, as conceived by Dion Fortune.

However, the novel is useful in portraying the kind of inner feelings and realisations that may pass within the minds and souls of the participants of the rite to make it a powerful and meaningful magical experience – and possibly any others present with minds tuned to pick up and to contribute to the inner proceedings. This would certainly be the case in terms of a group working of trained initiates – perhaps less so if performed as a spectacle before an audience.

Much of it can be picked up, however, by the lone reader who undertakes a formal meditational reading of it, either identifying with one of the participants, or perhaps best to begin with, simply as an observer of the rite. Ritual scripts, like theatre scripts, require a particularly concentrated method of study. Not of the intellect, but of the pictorial imagination, taking it all in slowly and deeply. Then what may appear banal or repetitive on the printed page can come across as a powerful subjective and even mystical experience.

✒ THE RITE OF PAN ✒

[The people being seated, the door keeper of the House of the Gods speaks to them.]

DOOR KEEPER: Those who come to a rite of Pan come to an ancient and forgotten worship, known in the childhood of man.

I invite you to come with me upon a journey. Leaving behind the ways of men, we go by a grassy track winding upward to the hills. The white farms and walled orchards grow fewer, and the woods begin.

We enter a thick wood of oak and fir, with laurel in the glades. We go through shade over moss, and the odour of leaves is in the air. As we pass onwards through the woods, the sound of the syrinx begins, faint and far, the pipe-call of Pan.

For we go to worship Pan in Arcady, and he calls through the woods as we come.

[The pipe-call of Pan is heard in the distance.]

PRIEST: Eva Evoe, Io Iacchos. Eva Evoe, Io Pan, Pan.

[The bell is struck, three and three.]

[The priestess, beside the door, sings.]

PRIESTESS: Strikes the bell and shines the light,
                Telling all who wake by night
                That the door without a key
                Is the opening on Arcady.

[Bell is struck three and three. A light shines in at the open door of the Temple.]

PRIESTESS: Shines the light and strikes the bell,
                Calling to the ritual

> All who love the Great God Pan,
> Half a goat and half a man.

[Bell struck three and three.]

PRIESTESS: Come all ye who long to flee
To the vales of Arcady.
For unto the world of men
The Great God Pan is come again.

[The procession enters to the slow beat of the bell, three times three.]
[Meditation.]
[Gong struck once.]

HIGH PRIEST: Let us formulate the Temple of Pan.

[Performs the Invoking Pentagram of Earth, piercing each star with the words IO PAN.]
[At the conclusion, facing East, draws [?] in air, raising arms in invocation, chanting.]

HIGH PRIEST: Eva Evoe, Io Iacchos. Eva Evoe, Io Pan, Pan.

The Temple of Pan is in the heart of his woods. A path winds through the thickets and leads to a grassy glade starred with flowers. At the far end, against the dark trees, is a semi-circle of white columns supporting a plinth. In the centre stands an altar to the god whereon are ranged the offerings sacred to him – honey, corn, and milk in oaken bowls, and wine in an earthen jar. The procession of worshippers winds through the woods, singing as they come.

[The priest and priestess rise and salute each other. He holds the earthen jar and she holds the oaken bowl. The priestess faces North, lifts the cup in salutation and cries:]

PRIESTESS: Eva Evoe, Io Iacchos.

[The priest lifts the jar in salutation and cries:]

PRIEST: Io Pan, Pan, Io Pan.

[Priest replaces jar on altar.]

PRIESTESS: Bowl of oak and earthen jar,
Honey of the honey-bee.
Milk of kine and Grecian wine,
Golden corn from neighbouring lea –
These our offerings, Pan, to thee,
Goat-foot god of Arcady.

[They half-circle the altar, changing places.]

PRIESTESS: Hornèd head and cloven hoof,
Fawns who seek and nymphs that flee;
Piping clear that draweth near
Through the vales of Arcady.
These the gifts we have of thee,
God of joyous ecstacy.

[They half-circle the altar, returning to their original places.]

PRIESTESS: Come, Great Pan, and bless us all;
Bless the corn and honey-bee.
Bless the vine and bless the kine,
Bless the vales of Arcady.
Bless the nymphs that laugh and flee,
God of all fertility.

[Places bowl on the altar.]

PRIEST: *[Raising jar in invocation]* Behold, thy vine is not barren, Pan.

We bring the first-fruits to thee, Great Pan.
Corn of the earth that thou lovest, Pan.
Milk of the beasts that thou leadest, Great Pan.
Accept our offerings, beloved Pan.
Io Pan, Io Pan, Io Pan, Pan.

[Places jar on altar.]

PRIESTESS: Eva Evoe, Io Iacchos. Eva Evoe, Io Pan, Pan.

PRIEST: Thy goat-hoofs ring on the rocks above us, Pan.
We hear the distant fluting through the trees, Great
Pan, Io Pan.

PRIESTESS: There is a stir of horned beasts at thy passing Pan.
The eyes of thy light-foot fawns look out from the
brakes, Great Pan, Io Pan.

PRIEST: The music comes over the hill, and the birds are
calling Pan.
Thy flowers gleam like stars in the dew-drenched
grass, Great Pan, Io Pan.

PRIESTESS: Syrinx calls from the distant river, Pan.
We hear the splash of thy following feet, Great Pan,
Io Pan.

PRIEST: There is a far singing in thy meadows, Pan.
White feet drum on thy sunlit lawns, Great Pan. Io
Pan.

PRIESTESS: We thy lost people come back to thy altars, Pan.
Long have we wandered with strangers not of our
blood, Great Pan, Io Pan.

PRIEST: Now seek we afresh our father and come again to
thy places, Pan.
Fill us and fire us with life that we once knew of old,
Great Pan, Io Pan.

PRIESTESS: Eva Evoe, Io Iacchos. Eva Evoe, Io Pan, Pan.

[Priest and priestess salute each other and return to their places.]

HIGH PRIEST: Let us call upon the Great God Pan with an adoration so fierce that it shall beget a sorcery within the cry. Let us waken the ancient faith again; and the Great God shall return to dwell with men.

[The priestess advances to the altar and raises her hands in invocation. The priest remains in meditation.]

PRIESTESS: O Great God Pan, return to earth again.
Come at my call, and show thyself to men.
Shepherd of goats, upon the wild hill's way
Lead thy lost flock from darkness unto day.
Forgotten are the ways of sleep and night;
Men look for them whose eyes have lost the light.
Open the door – the door that hath no key –
The door of dreams, whereby men come to thee –
Shepherd of goats, O answer unto me.

PRIEST: *[Stands.]* Eva Evoe, Io Iacchos. Eva Evoe, Io Pan, Pan.

[Priest advances to the altar and raises his hands in evocation.]

PRIEST: O thou whose infinite desire begat the worlds,
O thou whose dances men and gods must needs follow,
O thou re-arisen from the earth as thy bride from the sea,
Great Pan, we invoke thee!

Earth trembles at thine approaching feet,
The woods are hushed, and our hearts melt in thy sweet panic;
O thou master of the ancient springs of our being,
Great Pan, we invoke thee!

HIGH PRIEST: Eva Evoe, Io Iacchos. Eva Evoe, Io Pan, Pan.

PRIESTESS: We, thy lost people, come back to thy altars, Pan.
Rouse, O sleeping Pan, and come back to thy people,
Pan
> Io Pan, Io Pan, Pan.

I am thy priestess and bride, come unto me, Pan.
Fill me and fire me with life that I once knew of old,
Great Pan.
> Io Pan, Io Pan, Pan.

Thy breezes lift the tendrils of my hair, Pan.
Thy fires are stirring in my singing blood, Great Pan.
> Io Pan, Io Pan, Pan.

My feet drum thy lawns in the dances, Pan.
Mine are the flying white limbs thou seekest, Great
Pan.
> Io Pan, Io Pan, Pan.

I am the waiting earth that calleth, Pan.
I am the crescent moon that draweth thee, Great
Pan.
> Io Pan, Io Pan, Pan.

I am thy priestess and bride, come unto me, Pan.
Follow me, and thy people shall follow thee, Great
Pan.
> Io Pan, Io Pan, Pan.

[The priest and priestess salute each other, circle the altar, and return to their seats.]

HIGH PRIEST: Within every man there is a hidden god of elemental power: this we name the Pan Within. We call it forth to visible manifestation by the power of the name of the shepherd god of Arcady. Prepare ye now for the coming of the god!

[The priest comes to the altar. Priestess remains seated.]

PRIEST:
By the winds of the tempests that rush through thy
woods,
By the roar of thy torrents, descending in floods,
By the cry of thy beasts as the spring fires awoke,
    Great Pan of the powers, we invoke, we invoke!

By bright eyes in thy brakes and swift feet on thy
lawns,
By thy hushed August noons and grey sheen of thy
dawns,
The fierce joy in our veins that thy wine-fires awoke –
    God, bull, goat, and ram, we invoke, we invoke!

PRIESTESS: *[Coming up to altar.]*
Came the voice of Destiny
Calling by the Ionian Sea –
"The Great God Pan is dead, is dead.
Humbled is the hornèd head!
Shut the door that hath no key.
Waste the vales of Arcady."

Shackled by the Iron Age,
Lost the woodland heritage,
Heavy goes the heart of man,
Parted from the light-foot Pan.
Wearily he wears the chain
Till the goat-god comes again.

Half a man and half a beast,
Pan is greatest, Pan is least.
Pan is all, and all is Pan;
Look for him in everyman!
Goat-hoof swift and shaggy thigh,
Follow him to Arcady.

He shall wake the living dead.
Cloven hoof and hornèd head,
Human heart and human brain –

> Pan the goat-god comes again.
> Half a beast and half a man –
> Pan is all and all is Pan.
> Come O goat-god, come again!

PRIEST: His people call and the great god comes! Behold, he overshadows me. My body becomes his body, potent and perfect. He possesses my body, my body is his.

My blood becomes his blood, leaping and burning in my veins. He possesses my blood. My blood is his.

My brain becomes as his brain – filled with his fiery beauty, bursting with his exultant joy. He possesses my brain. My brain is his.

I am Pan! I am Pan! I am Pan!

PRIESTESS: Eva Evoe, Io Iacchos. Eva Evoe, Io Pan, Pan.
I am she who ere the earth was formed
Was Ea Binah Ge.
O first begotten Love, come unto me,
And let the worlds be formed of me and thee.

Giver of vine, and wine, and ecstasy.
God of the garden, shepherd of the lea;
Bringer of fear, who maketh men to flee,
I am thy priestess, answer unto me!

PRIEST: The god you sought for is dead, I am Pan.
The heavens are empty. Look down. I am he, Pan.

PRIESTESS: Io Pan.

PRIEST: White bull that roamed forth from my heaven was I, Pan.
Black goat that was born of my earth was I, Pan.

PRIESTESS: Io Pan.

PRIEST: The white ram returns to his kingdom, it is I, Pan.

Behold, I am goat, god, and ram. I am Pan.
I am come, the Great God Pan
Half a beast and half a man,
Rooted in life's deepest deep
God of Terror, Dark, and Sleep
Of deep full red 'neath forest trees
Of craggy paths and woodland leas.
Of joyous dance and ecstasy
In green cool glades of Arcady
Where the nymphs join in the dance
Shy – but kindling at my glance.
God of passion strong and full
The fierce swift strength of forest bull.
O Titaness of Earth awake
And that ancient passion slake
That begot the gods and men
The ancient fires wake again!

PRIESTESS: Io Pan.

PRIEST: Where the white feet flee through the woodland, there am I, Pan.
Where the green corn springs on my hills, it is I, Pan.

PRIESTESS: Io Pan.

PRIEST: Wherever life stirs with desire, it is I, Pan.
Laughing, insatiable, free, free as I am. I, Pan.

PRIESTESS: Io Pan.

PRIEST: I bring my wine and my honey, blessings of Pan.
Follow my wanton fawns, follow me – Pan.

PRIESTESS: Io Pan.

PRIEST: Drink who dares of my cup, fire of me, Pan.
Sip who dares of my sweets, desire of me, Pan.

PRIESTESS: Io Pan, Eva Evoe, Io Iacchos. Eva Evoe, Io Pan, Pan.

[Advancing towards altar.]

> I am Kypris, I am she.
> All men answer unto me.
> I awake the living Pan
> In the heart of every man.
> The god of fear, who makes men flee,
> Cometh unto thee and me.

[The priest and priestess quarter-circle the altar.]

PRIESTESS: Priest of Pan, arise and come.
Hear the goat-god call us home
Leaping on from rock to rock,
Pan the shepherd leads his flock,
By the ways of sleep and night
Upwards to the mountain-height.
I who call and ye who come,
Pan the shepherd leads us home.

[The priest and priestess quarter-circle the altar.]

PRIEST: Follow, then, the paths of Pan.
Thou art maiden, I am man.

TOGETHER: By the door that hath no key
Let us enter Arcady.

[The priest and priestess quarter-circle the altar.]

PRIEST: Who are ye who seek my places?

PRIESTESS: Thy lost children, Pan.

PRIEST: What seek ye?

PRIESTESS: Thy lost blessing, Pan.

PRIEST: Will ye dare it?

PRIESTESS: I have dared it, Pan.

> I am the star that rises from the sea,
> The twilight sea.
> O first begotten love, come unto me,
> And let the worlds be born of me and thee.
>
> Lo, I receive the gift thou bringest me –
> Life and more life in fullest ecstacy.
> I am the moon, the moon that draweth thee.
> I am the waiting earth that needeth thee.
> > Come unto me, Great Pan, come unto me!
> > Come unto me, Great Pan, come unto me!

[The High Priest goes to the altar and pours wine from the jar into the bowl. The priest and the priestess advance to meet each other across the altar, and he gives her to drink. They go to the curtain. The High Priest and the priestess draw back the curtain. The priest holds out the bowl towards the people.]

PRIEST: Ye are my people. Receive my gifts.
> To those strong to follow me, Life.
> To those weak to fear me, Death.
> To ye who dare it – the eyes to see Pan.
> To ye who dare it – strength to be Pan.
> > Receive my gifts.
>
> Earth of my hills to bear ye.
> Wind of my woods to stir ye.
> Sun of my noons to fire ye.
> Dew of my nights to cool ye.

Behold! I make you free of my kingdom. By your feet and your voices shall my people know when ye pass through my hidden places, and at sound of your laughter shall men break their fetters and follow.

PRIESTESS: Eva Evoe, Io Iacchos. Eva Evoe, Io Pan, Pan.

PRIEST: *[Raising hand in invocation.]* May the power of Pan be upon you.

[They drop the curtain and return to form the Triangle about the altar. The High Priest receives the bowl from the priest and replaces it upon the altar, after draining the bowl. All three return to seats.]

HIGH PRIEST: The door that hath no key is the door of the inward-looking eye. The Great God Pan awakes in the heart. The vales of Arcady are the free hills where he roams at will, forgotten of the Iron Age.

[Making the banishing pentagram of Earth.]

May the Great God Pan return to his place. Peace to all beings.

Let those who have seen the high rite of the great god return silently to their homes to meditate upon the mysteries. Let those who will send a record to the Temple of that which they have perceived.

[The lights are extinguished and the people withdraw.]

4
THE SEA PRIESTESS,
MOON MAGIC & THE RITE OF ISIS

In *The Sea Priestess* Dion Fortune introduced her most powerful and iconic female character, Vivien Le Fay Morgan. What is more, almost the whole of her Rite of Isis is included, albeit in fragments rather than a consecutive script.

As in the previous novels, Dion Fortune provides a considerable amount of esoteric theory and tradition in the course of the book as the sea priestess instructs her trainee priest. Much of it in this case concerning Atlantean traditions, which she uses to build up a magnetic relationship by reference to possible links in a previous incarnation. This indeed was also part of the mechanism in *The Goat-Foot God* and, as will later appear, in *Moon Magic*. Whether such connections are true or false, mutual belief in them can certainly strengthen a magical partnership. They are, in a sense, stage props to the dramatic action. As was said by Lewis Carroll's Bellman in *The Hunting of the Snark*, "If I say something three times it is true!" and at a magical level this is an important principle, otherwise expressed in the traditional adage "Fantasy is the ass that carries the Ark."

Apart from including various extracts from Dion Fortune's Rite of Isis the novel is particularly valuable for its description of the inner experiences of the male protagonist, as the story is recounted in his words. He also provides some interesting remarks on the type of chanting employed by the sea priestess.

"Then, too, Morgan sang to me. I never knew before that she could sing. Her singing was like nothing else that I have ever heard; it was half-way between folk-song and jazz, rising and falling by quarter-tones, and very rhythmical. And her songs were not like any other songs, either, being hymns to the old gods and the chants of the priests. Moreover her pitch was not the modern pitch at all, but in between, so that at first it sounded curiously flat and out of tune; but as one's ear became accustomed to the strange intervals, one realised that it was true music after its kind and that it spoke direct to the subconscious."

This presumably was also the technique employed by Dion Fortune, who gave demonstrations of it in some of her lectures, as we have seen. In this respect it is possible that the subconscious response, or the more direct conscious response, might not be always that which was hoped for, as has been reported by one or two fairly casual visitors to an evening lantern lecture where this type of chanting was demonstrated. However, there are others who can vouchsafe that it can be, for those duly prepared, a very powerful experience indeed, as Wilfred goes on to describe.

"And she sang it, not with the full singing voice of the concert singer, nor yet with the wail of a crooner, but with a mantric chanting, not loud, but a pure resonant tone that to me was very beautiful, and the rhythm in it was like the beat of the sea. And there were times when there came into her voice a strange inhuman timbre, curiously metallic, and when this came there was a change of consciousness, and she was someone else."

It was through this that he learnt something of the secret of magical images and their use, for borne away on the wings of her song, she became what she imagined herself to be, and he is drawn into the vision, to see her as a sea-priestess of Atlantis standing before him, "Morgan Le Fay, the foster daughter of Merlin, learned in all his lore."

This is obviously the consequence of a prepared build up, or "tuning of consciousness" through the medium of psychic experiments that they have been conducting with a crystal ball and by other means, arguably with a large mixture of arbitrary symbol making – for there are many other ways of looking upon Arthurian characters than the Atlantean background favoured by the sea priestess. Nonetheless, because believed in, at any rate for the purpose of the work in hand, it was none the less "subjectively objective" and highly effective, as the sea priestess herself goes on to explain at another point in their relationship.

> *"Sometimes I think one thing about myself, and sometimes I think another. As long as I believe in myself I find I can do certain things. If I ceased to believe in myself, I think I should just crumble to dust. There is more than one kind of truth. A thing that does not exist in our three dimensional world may exist in the fourth dimension and be real in its way ... I take mind as the fourth dimension, and find it works. That is good enough for me. ... You will never understand things until you trust them, for you inhibit what you doubt ... You will never know if the ice will bear unless you get onto it, never make custard without breaking eggs. I take my precautions and take my risks ... I don't pretend to understand them, but I know that they work."*

And she goes on to tell us a little of her ideas about herself and the principles of invocation from her point of view.

- That the gods are natural forces personified, and so to be made one with the gods is to become the channel of natural forces – which is not so rare as one might think.
- That devout men of all faiths have held that it is possible to bring the soul to a single-pointed focus by adoration and meditation and dedication; and that when this takes place, the god appears to come down and possess the worshipper, and the power of the god shines out from him (or her) like light from a lamp.
- That the ancients had known things about which we moderns have only just touched the fringe. The idea they had of priesthood was that it was a form of mediumship. Not that it was a personified god that spoke through the possessed and inspired priest or pythoness – a personified god is simply the way we represent spiritual powers to ourselves. We see the luminous countenance of the Eternal in the beautiful forms of the gods, and in this way we can learn more and do more than if we strive after abstract essences that elude us.

These principles can also apply to other forms of inner world contact apart from god forms. As Wilfred remarks:

> *"The Priest of the Moon had personality in a very marked degree and if he was the product of my subconscious, I am proud of it. There were times, not infrequent, when I used to wonder what he was, and whether I was deluding myself, or whether I was loopy; but each time I met him afresh I knew what he was, beyond all doubting, and he left his mark on me."*

Most of the words of the Rite of Isis are given in the novel, and a performance of it takes up most of chapter 25 in a place dedicated to the purpose that Wilfred has been decorating with sea pictures. For the occasion he wears a kind of kimono of coarse off-white shantung, silver painted sandals, a headdress or nemyss of silver lamé vaguely Egyptian in appearance, and a hooded cloak of dark indigo blue, fastened at the throat by a silver buckle in the shape of the sea-gods' sigil – a three-pronged trident. The heavy cloak was needed as part of his role was to walk the length of the down between the pylons at moon-rise to the temple in the seaside fort. Here he finds the sea priestess, clad in a close silvery robe, with a cloak of indigo gauze, and on her head the horned head-dress of the moon, bearing the lunar crescent of Isis.

The physical actions described are only relevant as far as the requirements of the plot of the novel go. What are more important are the realisations of Wilfred at the point in the rite that pertains to the evocation of the Persephone aspect of the goddess in the Rite of Isis.

At this point he realises the time has come when his life is poured out on the altar to give the goddess power, not in a violent and bloody rite, but as a slow ebbing away of strength, sinking down into a sleep that comes over him like a tide of the sea as it rises over the rocks outside. He is returning to the nothingness whence he had come, and life is ending as it had begun, in sleep.

He recalls the Biblical words – *'Or ever the silver cord be loosed, or the golden bowl be broken...'* and feels as if the golden bowl of his soul is being lifted up and poured out upon the moon-altar. Although he realises that on this occasion the silver thread is not loosed nor the golden bowl broken, for he still lives, although he might have come as near to death as a man might and yet return.

With the eyes of vision he sees the stars moving in their heavenly spaces and the tides in the earth-soul following them, like a tidal wave of the early seas following after the moon. Then the voice of the Priest of the Moon is heard in the role of the High Priest in the ritual, although the words given in the novel are not included in the script of the performed Rite of Isis as we have it – probably because the explanation was considered superfluous in the circumstances.

Our Lady is also the Moon, called of some Selene, of others, Luna, but by the wise Levanah, for therein is contained the number of her name. She is the ruler of the tides of flux and reflux. The waters of the Great Sea answer unto her, likewise the tides of all earthly seas, and she ruleth the nature of woman.

But there is likewise in the souls of men a flowing and an ebbing of the tides of life, which no one knoweth save the wise; and over these tides the Great Goddess presides under her aspect of the Moon. She comes from the sea as the evening star, and the magnetic waters of earth rise in flood. She sinks as Persephone in the western ocean and the waters flow back into the inner earth and become still in that great lake of darkness wherein are the moon and stars reflected. Whoso is still as the dark underworld life of Persephone sees the tides of the Unseen moving therein, and knoweth all things. Therefore is Luna called the giver of visions.

The voice ceases, and Wilfred thinks it is the end, until he sees in the utter darkness light moving like a tide, and he knows that even death has a manner of life of its own. It seems to him that he is looking out over the dark lake of the underworld to where Persephone sits on her throne awaiting his coming. He remembers that the sacrifice must go to his death without struggling, for the sacrifice must be consummated by unreserved dedication – and he wills to cross the dark water and come to her.

Thus he finds himself in the strange, high-prowed Egyptian boat of the gods called Millions of Years, wherein Osiris voyages, for he *is* Osiris. Beside him are the gods that travel with him, that are also his other selves. Horus, the hawk of the morning, is look-out in the bow, and Toom, god of the gathering dusk, sits silent in the stern; and at his feet is the Kephra Beetle, symbol of the sun at midnight, holding the emblem of time that is past. And so they travel over the dark waters of the lake of the underworld to come to the Queen of the Dead, his magical bride.

But as he draws toward her, the light increases, until it becomes the light of the room at the fort, and at the far end of which he sees the sea priestess sitting.

As he looks, she seems to begin to change from silver into gold, and a glowing aura of all the colours of the rainbow spring out around her. Her sleeping eyes open into an amazing animation of life, and she glows with life like a glorious dawn. Then the tide, that has flowed from him to her, turns and flows back from her to him, and he feels his life returning to him, but different. It has been made one with the life of the Goddess.

Now she sings, much the same song as in the final words of the Priestess in the Rite of Isis, identifying herself as Isis.

> *I am the star that rises from the sea*
> > *The twilight sea.*
> *I bring men dreams that rule their destiny.*
> *I bring the dream-tides to the souls of men;*
> *The tides that ebb and flow and ebb again*
> > *These are my secret, these belong to me.*
>
> *I am the eternal Woman, I am she!*
> *The tides of all men's souls belong to me.*
> *The tides that ebb and flow and ebb again;*
> *The silent, inward tides that govern men*
> > *These are my secret, these belong to me.*
>
> *Out of my hands he takes his destiny.*
> *Touch of my hands confers polarity.*
> *These are the moon-tides, these belong to me —*
> > *Hera in heaven, on earth, Persephone;*
> > *Levanah of the tides, and Hecate.*
> > *Diana of the Moon, Star of the Sea*
> > *Isis Unveiled and Ea, Binah, Ge!*

In the novel Morgan then rises, leaves the temple and goes out onto the forecourt which is by now flooded with moonlight. She stands for a moment before moving down the steps that lead to the point, with nothing between her and the sea, down to the very end where a flat table of rock lies just below the surface. He can only just see her now in her silver robes against the silver glitter of the sea. Then a cloud crosses the moon and when it is gone a light mist is coming in from the sea in long drifts, and he can no longer distinguish her through the haze.

His first instinct is to go after her to see if she is safe but a strong inner compulsion prevents him. And so he sits and waits, until he feels the presence of the Priest of the Moon come upon him – with a sense of awe and stimulation that one may feel in the presence of the dynamic personality of "one of the great of the earth". The words of the Priest of the Moon in the novel must come from the same source of inspiration as the words of the High Priest in the Rite of Isis, for they explain, amongst other things, the significance of the repeated mantram of **Ea, Binah, Ge,** as also **Marah.**

Thrice-greatest Hermes graved on the Smaragdine Tablet: "As above, so below." Upon earth we see the reflection of the heavenly principles in the actions of men and women.

All the gods are one god, and all the goddesses are one goddess, and there is one initiator.

In the beginning was space and darkness and stillness, older than time and forgotten of the gods. The sea of infinite space was the source of all being; life arose therein like a tide in the soundless sea. All shall return thereto when the night of the gods draws in. This is the Great Sea, **Marah,** *the Bitter One, the Great Mother. And because of the inertia of space ere movement arose as a tide, she is called by the wise the passive principle in nature, and is thought of as cosmic water, or space that flows.*

She is called by many names by many men; but to all she is the Great Goddess — space and earth and water. As space she is called **Ea,** *parent of the gods that made the gods; she is more old than time; she is the matrix of matter, the root-substance of all existence, undifferentiated, pure. She is also* **Binah,** *the Supernal Mother, that receiveth Chokmah, the Supernal Father. She is the giver of form to the formless force whereby it can build. She is also the bringer-in of death, for that which has form must die, outworn, in order that it may be born again to fuller life. All that is born must die, but that which dies shall be reborn. Therefore she* is called **Marah**, *the Bitter One, Our Lady of Sorrows, for she is the bringer-in of death.*

Likewise she is called **Ge**, *for she is the most ancient earth, the first-formed from the formless. All these is she, and they are seen in her, and whatsoever is of their nature answers unto her and she hath dominion over it. Her tides are its tides, her ways are its ways, and whoso knoweth the one, knoweth the other.*

Whatsoever ariseth out of nothingness, she giveth it; whatsoever sinketh down into nothingness, she receiveth it. She is the Great Sea whence life arose, to which all shall return at the end of the aeon.

Herein do we bathe in sleep, sinking back into the primordial depths, returning to things forgotten before time was, and the soul is renewed, touching the Great Mother. Whoso cannot return to the primordial hath no roots in life, but withereth as the grass. These are the living dead, who are orphaned of the Great Mother.

Finally he hears the Priest of the Moon speak to him by name, announcing that he will later return, for the work is not yet finished.

Wilfred never sees Morgan again, who vanishes mysteriously, but her work is later continued by Molly Coke, a local girl whom he has married, and who has been gifted with Morgan's star sapphires, with instructions on how to become a priestess of Isis. Her performance is described in the all-important ritual that closes the book.

It begins when the door of Wilfred's room opens soundlessly and Molly enters to take her stand at the foot of the bed. About her neck and on her wrists she wears Morgan's sapphires, and with the moonlight shining through the window behind her and thence through her diaphanous robes she appears like an ancient statue of Venus, holding out her arms towards him in the strange stiff attitude of the old gods, like Hathor when she appeared as a hawk. She begins to sing, using Morgan's tune, but the song is not one that Morgan has ever sung – indeed it is one that ends up with an invocation to Pan!

I am the Star that riseth from the sea,
The twilight sea.
All tides are mine, and answer unto me –
Tides of men's souls and dreams and destiny –
Isis Veiled and Ea, Binah, Ge.

Lo, I receive the gifts thou bringest me —
Life and more life — in fullest ecstasy!
I am the Moon, the Moon that draweth thee.
I am the waiting Earth that calleth thee.
Come unto me, Great Pan, come unto me!
Come unto me, Great Pan, come unto me!

The low ceiling of the room fades under the magic of her singing, opening out as a sea of stars under which they stand in a vast moonlit plain of bare black basalt, barren and volcanic. He thinks of lost Atlantis after the cataclysm and the mountains of the moon. In the centre of the plain is a moon temple of open black columns set in a circle like a slender and graceful Stonehenge of Doric pillars. Silhouetted against it are the lovely lines of Molly's figure, and Wilfred knows that she is exercising her ancient right and giving him the mating call in the name of the moon. And he sees why Morgan had said that, on the inner planes, the woman is positive, and should take the initiative, for the astral plane is ruled by the moon, and woman is her priestess, and when she comes in her ancient rite, representing the moon, the moon power is hers and she can fertilise the male with vitalising magnetic force.

It recalls a remark once made by the sea priestess. *'There is a commonplace relationship which you can have with any female of the species, and there is a subtle, magical relationship that is very rare. Which do you prefer?"*

It is the call of Aphrodite, the Awakener. And an answering power awakes in him from the depths of his being, far deeper than the outflow of desire that comes from a physical pressure. For she calls up from him reserves of vital force and brings them into action – reserves that the law of nature preserves for great crises when we fight for life itself – that give the madman his strength and the poet his creative frenzy. Not until these things are called up by the call of the beloved can we be said to have mated to the depths of our being. They are not called forth when a man woos a woman simply because he feels like it, but only when she comes to him in the name of Great Isis and bids him worship the goddess within her and through her.

The dark plain with its pillared temple grows clearer and clearer as if at moon-rise while Molly remains, a silvery figure in the silver moonlight – Isis Unveiled, come down from heaven to him, for she is made one with Her.

They have passed into another dimension – a dimension of the things of the mind. That which is between them has taken on a significance which is no longer personal but is part of Life itself – of Life going on in the Eternal Becoming. Molly is not simply a woman, but the power behind all women. And as he realises this, life comes in with such a rush that they are whirled away like leaves in the wind. The barriers of personality go down, and they are made one with cosmic life. Not one with each other, but one with a larger whole. But as things which are equal to a third are equal to each other, by losing themselves in the larger life so they find each other.

It is a thing difficult to explain, being a matter of experience. Something beyond the comradeship to be found in marriage. Something that the personality of the beloved cannot give. A magnetic something that begins to flow when we reach out beyond the personality of a woman towards her essential femininity. An essence, a vital principle, that creates the form through function, which the ancients personified as the Great Goddess Isis, veiled in heaven and unveiled in love.

And through all the ecstasy of the experience, like a muted orchestra accompanied by great singing, comes the voice of the Priest of the Moon presiding over the rite.

Learn now the mystery of the ebbing and flowing tides. Isis of Nature waiteth the coming of Her Lord the Sun. She calls Him; She draws Him from the place of the dead, the kingdom of Amenti, where all things are forgotten. And He comes to Her in His boat called Millions of Years, and the earth grows green with springing grain. For the desire of Osiris answers unto the call of Isis, and so will it ever be in the hearts of men, for thus the gods have formed them.

As the sound of the voice goes on they find themselves once more within the circle of slender black pillars that form the temple of the moon in the midst of the burnt-up, barren plain. The moonlight is concentrated within it, leaving all else in darkness.

For a while there is silence. Then the great tides of the skies rise up, to go by in a rhythm of musical colours, each with its own beat and note and periodicity, like the notes of an organ amid wheeling beams of light. One could conceive them as forces, or personify them as angels, with the glimpse of half-seen Faces as the great Forms go by on strong wings, singing as they pass.

Then they are alone once more, in the open temple in the empty plain, with only the moon above them and the whirling earth beneath, for all sacraments end in silence. Even the Priest of the Moon withdraws to leave them alone with the Moon and the Earth and Space.

Then they hear far off the sound of a rising tide, the soft silvery beat of light surf on shingle, and know that the waters are spreading over the earth at the end of an aeon. And the voice of the Priest of the Moon comes again as the sea draws nearer.

> *Consummatum est. Those who have received the touch of Isis have received the opening of the gates of the inner life. For them the tides of the moon shall flow and ebb and flow and never cease in their cosmic rhythm.*
>
> *The great sun, moving through the heavenly houses, has left the House of the Fishes for the House of the Water-bearer. In the coming age shall humanity be holy, and in the perfection of the human shall we find the humane. Take up the manhood into Godhead, and bring down the Godhead into manhood, and this shall be the day of God with us; for God is made manifest in Nature, and Nature is the self-expression of God.*

Moon Magic

Moon Magic acts as a sequel to *The Sea Priestess* and continues the story of Vivien Le Fay Morgan, but who now calls herself Lilith Le Fay, setting up a magical temple for herself in London, that overlooks not the sea, but the River Thames as seen from its south bank. She gives a detailed description of the furnishings of her temple, but says that it is all very simple, no magical names or numbers, save for the planetary symbols, no colours save black and silver – just the essentials of ceremonial magic, tartly adding *"minus all the trappings that are needed to impress the imagination of those who do not know what magical working really is."*

For whatever the layout of the physical temple, the important work takes place on an inner temple that overshadows it, which is built on the astral ethers by the magical imagination. It is approached by means of an imaginary journey, technically called a Composition of Mood or Composition of Place – the two terms are virtually synonymous – and she describes her method for doing this in company with her new priest.

They visualise themselves in Egypt, beside the Nile. It is moonlight, the moon full, with mist rising from the water. They approach a great pylon gate, its shadow black on the sand, and entering its shadow, pass through the great dark arch into the Court of the Lotus-pool, where the moonlight falls on pools where lotuses lie sleeping. Passing beside it, they climb some steps across a wide terrace, at the top of which a great door stands open, leading into a dark and lofty hall, lit only by a hanging lamp. This is the Hall of the Sphinxes and facing them is a dark curtain veiling the Holy of Holies. When the curtain parts the Goddess appears!

Not that this is a template for all temple working, as she remarks with characteristic hauteur: *"I cannot answer for what other occultists do, especially in fiction; nor do I always know why they do it, and I sometimes doubt if they do either; I can only answer for myself and those of my own Tradition."* It is the process of entering "the Door Without a Key" also called the Door of Dreams by which she says *"the sensitive escape into insanity when life is too hard for them, and artists use as a window in a watch-tower. Psychologists call it a psychological mechanism; magicians call it magic; and the man in the street calls it illusion or charlatanry according to taste. It does not matter to me what it is called, for it is effectual."*

She is obviously a rather spiky character with a high self regard who in another part of the book rather resents the impertinence of someone whom she regards as of a "less high grade" than herself. In many ways the less pretentious Mona Freeman of *The Goat-Foot God* and Molly Coke of *The Sea Priestess* might be said to be more rounded and pleasant human beings. However, Vivien or Lilith obviously knows what it is all about when it comes to performing a Rite of Isis.

In her work with Rupert Malcolm she describes vibrating *"the age old chant"* with corresponding movements of her hands and arms in signs that correspond to the words – the signs of sea and space and inner earth; of hailing Aphrodite and the chaste Diana of the moon; even the bat-wings of Hecate – for unless one can handle the dark aspect of a force, she says, one cannot handle the bright – and at the end she gives the full salute of a priest.

> *I am she who ere the earth was formed*
>> *Was Rhea, Binah, Ge.*
>> *I am that soundless, boundless, bitter sea,*
>> *Out of whose depths life wells eternally.*
>> *Astarte, Aphrodite, Ashtoreth,*
>> *Giver of Life and bringer-in of Death;*
>> *Hera in heaven, on earth Persephone;*
>> *Levanah of the Tides, and Hecate;*
>> *All these am I, and they are seen in me.*
> *The hour of the high full moon draws near;*
>> *I hear the invoking words, hear and appear —*
>> *Isis Unveiled, and Rhea Binah, Ge,*
>> *I come unto the priest that calleth me.*

She also describes her inner vision in the Persephone sequence. As she progresses into the working the room disappears for her, and she finds herself standing in a vast underground cave with dark water at her feet. She is no longer robed in the dull black velvet of the outer temple that fits all the negative forces but in soft, shimmering filmy indigo, blue and purple. On her head is the horned moon, about her hips the starry girdle of the constellations, and she knows that she is Isis in her underworld aspect, whom the Greeks called Persephone.

There is nothing of the human left about her. She is as vast as the universe, her head among the stars, her feet on the curve of the earth as it swings under her in its orbit. Around her, in translucent space, stand the stars, rank on rank, and she is of their company. Beneath her, very far beneath, all Nature lies spread like a green patterned carpet. Alone on the globe she soars through space, with the kneeling man before her, and there are no others in creation save he and her – the All-woman and the Archetypal Man, with the whole of the manifested universe summed up in the relationship between them.

> *"I was in my calm, negative, underworld aspect as Queen of the Dead, ruler of the Kingdoms of Sleep. In death men come to me across the dark river, and I am the keeper of their souls until the dawn. But there is also*

a death-in-life, and this likewise leadeth on to rebirth, for there is a turning-within of the soul whereby men come to Persephone.

"I am also the Great Deep, whence life arose, to which all shall return at the end of an aeon. Herein do we bathe in sleep, sinking back into the primordial deep, returning to things forgotten before time was, and the soul is renewed, touching the Great Mother. Whoso cannot return to the Primordial hath no roots in life — they are the living dead who are orphaned of the Great Mother.

"I was that Great One in her most benign aspect, tranquil, brooding, as a woman broods over her unborn child. I was the Giver of Sleep, blessing the weary man before me with my great gift. He had come back to me to be a child again, as an overwrought man always does, as he needs must do if he is to renew his strength to battle with life; for unless a woman can brood over him as I brooded over Malcolm that night, his nerves will wear bare of insulation as a frayed wire. It is only when, for love's sake, she can make him as the unborn, that he renews his strength, for to him she is the soul of earth wherein are his deepest roots. The more dynamic the man, the more dependent is he upon his earth-contacts in his woman.

"These are not the contacts of passion; they are older, more primal than that; they go back to the days when humanity was as yet unborn from the earth-soul. I was his anima, his underworld contact, his link with most ancient earth and things primordial wherein are the roots of strength; through me he could touch them as he was powerless to do alone, for man is of the sun and stars and fire; but woman is of dark space and dark earth and dark, primordial water."

These last phrases are also deeply spiritual Qabalistic working, for they describe the Supernal Spheres of the Tree of Life, Binah and Chokmah – the principles of Divine Understanding and of Divine Wisdom – the highest expression of the polar expression of the ultimate godhead of Kether – the Great Countenance – the Crown of Creation.

And these high principles are expressed in human terms as she sings the part of the Rite that she refers to as the Song of Compassion of Isis: "a strange song, begotten of magic; it is very old, and only priestesses can sing it."

The moon is riding high and clear,
O lovely one, draw near, draw near;
To lonely men on lonely ways
Come down in dream of silver haze.
Persephone, Persephone,
All in the end shall come to thee.

"*I was the archetypal woman with my Goddess behind me; and before me was he, the archetypal man, who needed me.*"

The end of the novel also provides us with an account of the inner experience of the priest in the performance of the rite.

"*He could feel the beginnings of the gathering of power. The magic was starting to work. He was in the place of the priest, and whatever this unknown force might be, it meant to work through him. He steadied himself and waited. Let it work! It was the only way. He needn't do anything. It was a natural force, and it would use him, its natural channel; all he need do was let it use him.*

"*He concentrated on the idea of passivity, of presenting an open channel to that which would come to him from behind, and through him to her. Great Nature was drawing near; the tide was rising along the appointed channel.*

"*Then, for the first time, he knew himself as part of Nature. Such a thing had never entered his head before, for all his study of comparative anatomy. He knew that, deep in him, was a level that had never been separated from the earth soul, just as the image of the primordial woman in the Black Temple had never been cut away from the living rock but was united to it along her back-bone, and he knew that he too, at the spinal level, belonged to Nature, and that through the channel of that hollow rod Nature would use him, and gave himself to Her power.*

"*Then in a flash he felt the levels coalesce; that which he had previously known as purely physical he felt to be spiritual as well. The force was rising from the spinal to the cerebral level and passing out of the province of physiology. Then he felt it lift level again, and pass out of the province of psychology into that which lies beyond. A vision of starry spheres seemed around him. The room had faded. Lilith had changed into Isis and he himself was the Nature-force rising up from primordial deeps to fertilise her! He was not a man, he was a force. He was part of the earth-life, and Nature was manifesting through him; and she, Lilith, was not a person either; she was the goal of the force — that was all. It was quite simple. The force had taken charge. There was no thought, no feeling, save the terrific pressure of force that used his organism as a channel of manifestation. The less of personality there was in this the better — let the force do its own work!*

"It was like being struck by lightning. The power came, and passed, and as its reverberations went rolling away into space, he saw as the clouds parted before his eyes the face of Lilith le Fay, but made young and lovely, and he gazed at her as Adam must have gazed at the newly-created Eve when he awoke from his deep sleep and found her beside him.

"The straight run-through of power had blown clear all the obstructions and blockings and tangles in his nature just as a choked channel is cleared by a force-pump. From level to level the power had risen, and cleared the channel as it went. He was a man utterly re-made. How, and by what, he could not say. He only knew that, exhausted and at peace, he was ready to sing with the morning stars as soon as his strength came back to him, and that his mind had the crystal lucidity of sunlit space."

At which point we might do well to reflect that there are two poles to the great circuit of force, which is why, in her Introduction to *Moon Magic*, Dion Fortune cites Lilith singing to a weary man: *"Forgotten are the ways of sleep and night..."*.

And so we might well echo the ending of that hymn of invocation:

Open the door, the door that hath no key —
The door of dreams whereby men come to thee.
Shepherd of goats, O answer thou me!

– which is actually from the Rite of Pan!

⚘ THE RITE OF ISIS ⚘

PRELIMINARY READING

HIGH PRIEST: The rites of the Green Ray are designed to restore to the soul of man that which was lost since the childhood of the race. By means of the joy of Beauty are the ancient forces awakened, and the soul of man is made whole that before was partial and imperfect.

LECTOR: Under the name of Isis we personify a mode of the manifestation of power – the feminine, latent and receptive mode. This we see as a trinity in unity: Binah, Persephone, and Aphrodite, three aspects of the feminine polarity.

As Binah, the Supernal Mother, she is primordial space, the source of all being; as Persephone, the Compassionate Mother, she is Queen of those that sleep; these two are negative and latent; but as Aphrodite, obedient to the laws of alternating polarity, she is positive and dynamic, a giver of life.

Under the form of the Three-fold Isis we represent the feminine Glyph of Life. All women are Isis, and Isis is all women. In her glyph are deep truths to be meditated upon.

All who participate in the rite as worshippers must play their part, each after their kind. All women should hear the voice of the priestess speaking for them; and all men should hear in the voice of the priest their own souls speaking. Likewise they should help with the inner eye the building of the Temple as the reading describes it.

When all is over, let those who will make a record of that which they have perceived or realised and send it to the Temple.

THE FORMULATION OF THE TEMPLE
[Colours: Black and Silver]

LECTOR: Learn now the secret of the web that is woven between the light and the darkness. Whose warp is life evolving in time and space, and whose weft is spun of the lives of men. Behold we arise with the dawn of time from the grey and misty sea, and with the dusk we sink in the Western ocean; and the lives of a man are strung like pearls on the thread of his spirit. And never in all his journey goes he alone, for that which is solitary is barren.

HIGH PRIEST: Be far from us O ye profane. Brethren of the Mysteries, we are about to invoke the descent of the power of Isis. To this end, let the Temple be sealed.

[High Priest opens Temple in the Name of Isis – "In the Name of Isis I open the East" etc.
When he finally faces East again, he raises his arms in invocation and says "Let the power of the Goddess extend through the Temple".]

LECTOR: The Temples of Isis are in sheltered places where the earth is fertile and the waters are pure. Isis is the Mother of all living; she is the Mate of the Male; enter her Temple with clean hands and a pure heart lest ye defile the source of Life. Be far from us O ye profane.

Those who adore the Isis of Nature adore her as Hathor with the horns upon her brow; but those who adore the celestial Isis know her as Levanah the Moon. She is also the Great Deep whence Life arose. She is all ancient and forgotten things wherein our roots are cast. Upon Earth she is ever-fecund; in heaven she is ever virgin. She is the Mistress of the Tides that flow and ebb and flow and never cease. In these things are the keys of her Mystery known to her initiated.

Isis is Our Lady of the Heavens and our Mother the Earth. She is all Goddesses men's hearts have worshipped, for these are not many things, but one thing under many forms. All the Gods are One God, and all the Goddesses are one Goddess.

The Temples of Isis are built of black marble and hung with

silver, and she herself sitteth veiled in the Innermost. Her symbol is the cup of pure water in whose depth is the moon reflected. Let us meditate on the Inner Temple.

[Temple Building. Silent meditation for two minutes. Bell is struck.]

HIGH PRIEST: The Temple being duly builded, let us consecrate the Priestess of Isis as our pythoness. *[Rising and raising arms in invocation]* O thou most holy and adorable Isis, who in the heavens art the Supernal Mother, and upon Earth our Lady of Nature, and in the astral kingdoms between heaven and earth the ever-changing Moon. Thee, Thee, we adore in the symbol of the Moon in her splendour ever-changing. And in the symbol of the deep sea that reflects her. And in the symbol of the opening of the gates of Life. We see thee crowned in silver in the heavens; and veiled in green upon the Earth; and in thy robe of many colours at the Gates. O heavenly Silver that answerest to the celestial Gold. O Green that risest from the Grey! O Rainbow Glory of Living! Come at my invocation and possess this priestess dedicated to thy service, that she may be to us the incarnation of the Goddess, and a pythoness of Revelation.

PRIESTESS: O Glorious Isis, Moon and Earth and Water, and all things negative and mutable, show forth thy form. O thou that sleepest in matter and awakenest in the ether, I offer unto thee the pythoness dedication. Speak with my lips; hear with my ears; touch with my hands; ray forth from me the subtle and mysterious life that was in the beginning.

[The priest comes up to the altar, extends his hands to project power upon the priestess, formulating the Goddess.]

PRIEST: O thou that wast before the earth was formed,
Rhea, Binah, Ge.
O tideless soundless, boundless, bitter sea,
I am the invoking priest, come to me.

O arching sky above and earth beneath,
Giver of life and bringer-in of death,

Persephone, Astarte, Ashtoreth,
I am the invoking priest, come unto me.

O golden Aphrodite, answer me;
Flower of the foam, rise from the wine-dark sea.
The hour of the high full moon draws near,
Hear the invoking words, hear and appear –
Shaddai El Chai and Rhea, Binah, Ge.

[Projects power on to priestess.]

PRIEST: O Isis veiled and Rhea, Binah, Ge.

PRIESTESS: I come unto the priest that calleth me.

PRIEST: The hour of the full moon tide draws near.

PRIESTESS: I hear the invoking words, hear and appear.

PRIEST: Shaddai El Chai and Rhea, Binah, Ge.

PRIESTESS: I come unto the priest that calleth me.

[Priestess projects power on to the priest.]

PRIESTESS: I am she who ere the earth was formed
Was Rhea, Binah, Ge.
I am that soundless, boundless, bitter sea,
Out of whose depths life wells eternally.
Astarte, Aphrodite, Ashtoreth,
Giver of Life and bringer-in of Death;
Hera in heaven, on earth Persephone;
Levannah of the Tides, and Hecate;
All these am I, and they are seen in me.
The hour of the high full moon draws near;

I hear the invoking words, hear and appear –
Isis Unveiled, and Rhea, Binah, Ge,
I come unto the priest that calleth me.

PERSEPHONE
[Colours: Blue, Silver, Black and Purple]

LECTOR: Be ye far from us, O ye profane, for the unveiling of the Goddess is at hand. Look not upon her with impure eyes, lest ye see your own damnation. The unregenerate and untaught man gazeth upon the face of Nature, and it is to him darkness of darkness, but the initiated and illuminated man gazeth thereon and seeth therein reflected the Luminous Image of the Creator. Be ye far from us O ye profane, while we adore God made manifest in Nature.

[Priestess goes to altar; stands there.]

PRIESTESS: I am the veiled Isis of the shadows of the Sanctuary
I am she that moveth as a shadow behind the tides of Death and Birth.
I am she that cometh forth by night and no man seeth my face.
I am older than time and forgotten of the gods.
No man may look upon my face and live,
For in the hour he parteth my veil, he dieth.

[Priest goes to the altar and lays his hands upon it.]

PRIEST: There is one man that looketh upon thy face.
Behold, I am the sacrifice.
I part thy veil and die to the birth.

HIGH PRIEST: The daughter of the Great Mother is Persephone, Queen of Hades, Ruler of the Kingdom of Sleep. At death men go to her across the Dark River, and she is the keeper of their souls until the Dawn. But there is also a death in life and this likewise leadeth on to re-birth, for there is a turning within of the soul whereby men come to Persephone.

She is also the Great Sea whence Life arose, to which all shall return at the end of an aeon. Herein do we bathe in sleep, sinking back into the primordial deep, returning to things forgotten before Time was; and the soul is renewed, touching the Great Mother.

Whosoever cannot return to the Primordial have no roots in Life. They are the living dead that are orphaned of the Great Mother.

There are two deaths by which men die, the greater and the lesser. The death of the body and the death of Initiation. And of these two, the death of the body is the lesser. The man who looks upon the face of Isis dies, for the goddess takes him.

He that would die to the birth, let him look upon the face of the goddess in this mystery. Be ye far from us, O ye profane, for one goes by the Path that leads to the Well-head beside the White Cypress.

PRIEST: *[Raising head and addressing Priestess.]*
Isis veiled, and Rhea, Binah, Ge,
Lead me to the well of memory –
The well-head where the pale white cypress grows –
By secret twilight paths that no man knows;
The shadowy path that dividing into three.
Diana of the Ways and Hecate;
Selene of the Moon, Persephone.
I see it now, the shadowy path appears
Wrapped in the gloom of immemorial years;
Veiled in the mists and shadows of all Time,
Soft, still and calm in solitude sublime.
And now appears the Well and Sacred Tree
Whereto come all who long for memory.
Thronged all about with shades of the dim past
Of pain and sorrow changed to joy at last.
The mists disperse, the shadows grow more bright
And through the glimmer falls thy pale soft light.
This way is not for one who goes alone;
Not to the loveless is the Well-head shown.
To search unscathed within its deepest deep
Both priest and priestess must the vigil keep.
Geburah joined to Chesed makes the path
On which the soul can mount to Daath.

O, Overlord of all the gods above
Great Eldest Brother, first-left, last-found Love.
In all our ways we claim Thy potent aid.
Who seek the Truth and seek it unafraid.

The high full moon in the mid-heaven shines clear,
O hear the invoking words, hear and appear –
Shaddai El Chai, and Rhea, Binah, Ge.

PRIESTESS: I am that soundless, boundless, bitter sea;
All things in the end shall come to me.
Mine is the kingdom of Persephone,
The Inner Earth where lead the Pathways Three.
Who drinks the waters of that hidden Well
Shall see the things whereof he dare not tell;
Shall tread the shadowy path that leads to me –
Diana of the Ways and Hecate;
Selene of the Moon, Persephone.

[The priest bends over the altar, resting his head and arms on it as if in sleep.]

PRIESTESS: I am that secret Queen Persephone;
All tides are mine and answer unto me.
Tides of the Airs, Tides of the Inner Earth;
The secret silent Tides of Death and Birth;
Tides of men's souls, and dreams of destiny –
Isis unveiled and Rhea, Binah, Ge.

Sink down, sink down, sinker deeper and sink deep
Into eternal and primordial sleep.
Sink down, sink down, be still and draw apart
Into the Earth's most secret heart.
Drink of the waters of Persephone,
The secret well beside the sacred Tree.
Waters of strength and life and inner Light
Primordial joy drawn from the deeps of night.
Then rise, made strong, with life and hope renewed,
Reborn from darkness and from solitude.
Blessed with the blessing of Persephone,
And secret strength from Rhea, Binah, Ge.

[Priest rises and receives the Priestess' salute. Both return to their seats.]

APHRODITE
[Colours: Green and Gold]

LECTOR: Learn now the mystery of the ebbing and flowing tides. That which is dynamic in the Outer is latent in the Inner, for that which is above is as that which is below, but after another manner.

Isis of Nature awaiteth the coming of her Lord, the Sun. She calls him: she draws him from the place of the Dead, the kingdom of Amenti where all things are forgotten. And he comes to her in his boat called Millions of Years, and the Earth grows green with the springing grain. For the desire of Osiris answers to the call of Isis. And so it will ever be in the hearts of men, for thus the gods have formed them. Whoso denieth this is abhorred of the gods. But in the heavens our Lady Isis is the Moon, and the Moon-powers are hers. She is also the Priestess of the Silver Star that rises from the twilight sea. Hers are the magnetic moon-tides ruling the hearts of men. In the Inner , she is all-potent. She is the Queen of the Kingdoms of Sleep. All the invisible workings are hers, and she rules all things ere they come to birth. Even as through Osiris her mate the Earth grows green with springing grain, so the mind of man conceives through her power. This secret concerns the inner nature of the goddess, which is dynamic. Let us show forth in a rite the dynamic nature of the goddess that the minds of men may be as fertile as the fields.

PRIEST: *[Coming up to the altar.]*
>O Isis veiled on earth but shining clear
>In the mid-heaven now the full moon draws near;
>Hear the invoking words, hear and appear.
>
>O evening star, rise from the twilight sea.
>Answer from Inner Earth, Persephone.
>Giver of life and bringer-in of death,
>Astarte, Aphrodite, Ashtoreth,
>Flower of the bitter foam, come unto me,
>Isis unveiled, and Rhea, Binah, Ge.

O Isis veiled on earth, but shining clear
In the mid-heaven now the full moon is near;
O hear the invoking words, hear and appear.

The lonely earth is hungering after thee.
Come in the night, give light that we may see,
O Isis of men's hearts, come unto me.

PRIESTESS: *[Advancing to altar.]*

I am the star that riseth from the sea,
    The twilight sea.
I bring men dreams that rule their destiny.
I bring the moon times to the souls of men;
The tides that flow and ebb and flow again;
These are my secret, these belong to me.
Hera in heaven, on earth Persephone.
Levannah of the Tides and Hecate.
Veiled Isis, Aphrodite from the sea,
All these am I, and they are seen in me.

I am the Eternal Woman, I am She.
The tides of all men's soul's belong to me;
The tides that flow and ebb and flow again,
The silent inward tides that govern men;
These are my secret, these belong to me.
Out of my hands man takes his destiny;
Touch of my hands confers serenity;
These are the Moon-tides, these belong to me,
Isis unveiled and Rhea, Binah, Ge.

PRIEST: O Thou whose power drew forth the Prime Mover
from the ancient stillness.
O Thou from whose body first Being began.
O Thou whose beauty moved Ptah on his throne to
desire.
By thy beauty and body we adore and invoke.

77

The desire of thy body put chains on his neck,
In pursuit of thy beauty did he make himself manifest.
O Thou whose desire is in all things that be –
By the power of thy beauty we adore and invoke.

By the power of Old Night, whence all sprang, we invoke Thee.
By the first mystic swirl in the stillness that told of Thy power, we invoke Thee.
By the net which Thou wovest to draw Ptah from his heaven, we invoke Thee.
By the kisses that smote him with death that the world might be born, we invoke Thee.
By thy merciful veil, by thy scourgings and pangs,
By thy sweet secret places, by midnight and moon,
By earth and by water – Isis, Light of the Heavens and Desire of the World –
I invoke,   I invoke,   I invoke!

LOTUS COURT

PRIEST: Persephone, O Queen of my desire!
Thy radiant Light fills me with soft moon-fire.
Persephone, Persephone,
Queen of the Night, I call for Thee.

In outer space the springs of being rise;
With tidal sweep life streams across the skies,
And in men's hearts awake the slumbering fires.
Thou art the Queen of Dreams and of Desires.
Persephone, Persephone,
Queen of the Night, I long for Thee.

O star-crowned Queen of Outer Space
Who holds vast worlds in thy embrace.
All who are loved and all who love
Bring down thy radiance from above,

Persephone, Persephone,
Whoso'er loves is one with Thee.

O Goddess Queen, draw gently near,
Thou whom all seek, Appear! Appear!
To lonely men on lonely ways
Come down in dreams of silver haze.
Persephone, Persephone,
All in the end shall come to Thee.

*[Priest and Priestess step back. High Priest drops the curtain and comes
to the altar.]*

HIGH PRIEST: Consummatum est. Those who have received the
Touch of Isis have received the opening of the gates of the Inner
Life. For them the tides of the Moon shall flow and ebb and flow in
their cosmic rhythm. To them that adore Isis, she brings tranquillity,
and to the favoured few she comes as in a dream.

Depart ye in silence to meditate upon the Mysteries, and let who
will send in a record to the Temple.

APPENDICES

1. Ceremonial Magic Unveiled
2. The Novels of Dion Fortune
3. The Winged Bull – a study in esoteric psychology
4. Occult Experience – the Establishment of the sphere of Yesod in the aura
5. Notes on "The Circuit of Force"
6. Inner teachings on Polarity, Trance Address, December 16th 1940
7. Recommended Reading

Appendix 1

CEREMONIAL MAGIC UNVEILED

By DION FORTUNE

An historically important article by Dion Fortune that appeared in the January 1933 issue of "The Occult Review", hailing two new books by Israel Regardie ("The Tree of Life" and "The Garden of Pomegranates") that effectively ended the culture of secrecy that had hitherto surrounded the "Golden Dawn" tradition of magic. Her own work "The Mystical Qabalah" was soon to follow, along with its related occult novels ("The Winged Bull", "The Goat-Foot God", "The Sea Priestess") and the semi-public celebration of her Rites of Isis and of Pan.

Gareth Knight

IF I read the signs of the times aright, the veil of the Temple of the Mysteries is being drawn back at the present moment. There are phases in the spiritual life of mankind just as there are weather cycles extending over periods of years, and the tide which began to move during the first decade of the twentieth century is gathering head as it proceeds. The signs of the times are to be seen in the publication of certain books on magic in which the genuine secrets are given, and given in a form available for any reader with a capacity for metaphysical thought. Among the most important of these are Israel Regardie's two books: *The Garden of Pomegranates* and *The Tree of Life*.

The Garden of Pomegranates, oddly enough, deals with the Tree of Life, the famous glyph of the Qabalists, which is used as a card-index system in which are filed all ideas concerning man and the Universe according to certain well-understood systems of association, and which, by means of the pattern of its arrangement, is used to discover the correspondences and relationships between them.

The Cabbala is increasingly being recognized as the basis of Western

Occultism. Anyone who wants to appreciate esoteric philosophy as taught in that system, and more especially anyone who wants to make practical use of it, whether in magic or meditation, needs a working knowledge of the Tree of Life. Information on this decidedly recondite subject has hitherto been to seek in a number of books, some of them rare and hard to come by, and many of them confused and elusive in their wording. Mr. Regardie has given, in a lucid and concise form, and Messrs. Rider have issued at a moderate price, a most admirable handbook on the technical system of the Tree. It is lucid, comprehensive and concise, and performs a very useful service in correlating the Cabbalistic, Eastern, and Egyptian systems. It is thus possible for the student to trace out the interrelation between the two systems which are worked together in the West, the Egyptian and Cabbalistic; and for the Theosophist to recognize the classification with which he is familiar, when it is applied to the glyph of the Tree in the technical methods of Western occultism.

Mr. Regardie has the inestimable advantage of knowing the Hebrew language; in this, as an occultist, he is unique; for although most occultists working the Western tradition have enough Hebrew to transliterate the Words of Power for inscription on pantacles and talismans or for numerological work, they number no Hebrew scholars among their ranks, but are all dependent on translations; even McGregor Mathers and Wynn Westcott did not translate from the original Hebrew, but from Latin versions, and they have saddled the Western schools with some tiresome errors of transliteration and pronunciation.

Mr. Regardie gives a classification of the Tree and the constitution of man according to the Cabbalists, and of the correspondences between them, which is much more lucid and illuminating even than that given by McGregor Mathers' admirable introductory essay to *The Kabbalah Unveiled,* for he gives the correspondences in terms of modern psychology as well as of metaphysics and the psychic states.

The sections of the book, however, which will be of chief interest to students of the occult, and which will cause bitter heartburnings in certain quarters, are his chapters on the attributions and correspondences of the Ten Holy Sephiroth and the Twenty-two Paths between them. These attributions have been among the special preserves of certain occult schools; but Mr. Regardie gives them, even to the jealously guarded secret of the correct attribution of the Tarot trumps. There will certainly be heartburnings!

Mr. Regardie does not specifically state his authorities, but it is unquestionably the system taught in the "Order of the Golden Dawn", founded by the late S. L. McGregor Mathers, that he is using. If I have been a Reheboam who has scourged occult secrecy with whips, Mr. Regardie is a Jeroboam who is using scorpions!

However, he has my unqualified blessing, for what it is worth to him. There is no legitimate reason that I have ever been able to see for keeping these things secret. If they have any value as an aid to spiritual development, and I for one believe that they have the highest value, there can be no justification for with-holding them from the world. The only reason of which I am aware, and one which I suspect of being a weighty one with those who have so long sat resolutely upon the lid of occult secrecy, is that for purposes of priestcraft and prestige a secret system is a useful weapon. A weighty reason, this, human nature being what it is, but not a justification in the eyes of those who have the welfare of humanity at heart.

It has always been the custom of the "Golden Dawn" to wrap itself in the utmost secrecy. To a certain extent this secrecy is unquestionably necessary, for many eminent people have at different times belonged to the Order, and they would not have dared to have done so if they could not have been sure of preserving the secret of their interest in matters occult. Consequently the strict secrecy concerning the names of members and the places of meeting was and always will be essential.

Secrecy is also necessary concerning initiation rites if they are to be psychologically effective; for they should have an element of surprise for the candidate; and the possession of their secrets, from which the rest of the world is excluded, builds up a group-mind out of the pooled mentalities of the initiated brethren according to certain well-understood psychological laws.

Secrecy concerning practical formulae of ceremonial magic is also advisable, for if they are used indiscriminately, the virtue goes out of them. All these formulae have unwritten astral workings attached to them; if they are used in ignorance by the uninitiated, and without the astral workings, the magnetism which has been worked up in the symbols is given off and not replaced; but when they are used by the trained occultist, who performs the astral workings with power, more magnetism is worked up than is given off, and the symbols become stronger. That is why the old formulae, which have been used by generations of trained adepts, are so extraordinarily powerful.

Beyond this I do not think occult secrecy ought to go, and I am certainly not prepared to assist it. It is not possible to keep back the tide. Save for the reservations regarding the actual rituals, the day of occult secrecy is over. Whosoever can profit by the teachings ought to have them.

Mr. Regardie handles, very wisely, the section of his book dealing with the ceremonial rites, for he gives the principles without the actual formulae. The only formula he gives in full is that of the Banishing Ritual of the Lesser Pentagram. I was at first inclined to quarrel with him for giving this, for one feels instinctively that a formula which is messed about by all and sundry will not long retain its value for anybody. But on second thoughts I am inclined to acquit him. It is this formula which is given to the student immediately on initiation, long before he is taught any practical working, in order that he may be in a position to protect himself in case of astral trouble. If Mr. Regardie is justified in drawing back the veil at all, then he is, undoubtedly, justified in providing the necessary protection against anything untoward that may come through that veil. The Lesser Pentagram is of the nature of a fire extinguisher, and it is very necessary to have some such device handy, when one adventures into such highly charged levels of the Unseen as are contacted by the methods he describes.

Now what is going to be the outcome of this general disclosure of the secrets of the Mysteries? As in most drastic happenings, the results will be mixed; but it is my belief that the good will far outweigh the evil. That some folk will burn their fingers experimenting with that which they do not understand I have no doubt, but on the whole the gain to serious students will be inestimable. Mr. Regardie has done his work admirably, both in the spirit and in the letter. *The Tree of Life* is a book which it would be difficult to praise too highly; it is going to be one of the classics of occultism.

When the secrets of the Mysteries are given forth in this manner and with this spirit, I, for one, decline to believe that they are either betrayed or profaned, but rather that the author is duly accredited to speak on behalf of Those who can bind or loose, irrespective of tradition or oaths of secrecy. It is a curious fact that this is the third book of its kind to become available at the present moment. I see from an article in the November number of this magazine that Foyle's are issuing Crowley's *Magick* in a cheap edition, thus rendering it available for the general student, who has probably never heard of, or could not afford to purchase, the privately printed edition which appeared in Paris a couple of years ago. The third person of this unholy trinity of revealers of the Mysteries is my humble self, who have been doing much the same thing as Mr. Regardie in a series of articles on the Cabbala which has been running in my own magazine, *The Inner Light*.

I know that I undertook this work under a strong inner compulsion that this teaching must now be given out to the world; that it was the will of those who held the keys that the door should be set open in these matters, and that we were about to enter on an entirely new phase of occult activity. So far as I can see, ceremonial magic is coming out into the open, as witness even the futile operations of Mr Harry Price on the Brocken, concerning which I had something to say in a previous issue of the *Occult Review*. One does not see sporadic manifestations of the same thing springing up here and there in entire independence; they come from a common source. This source I believe to be one of those high spring tides in things spiritual which, from time to time, visit our earth. For any organization to try and close the sluice-gates against it by oaths of secrecy, is to keep back the Atlantic with a broom.

It is, therefore, important for those who have knowledge of the subject to recognize the change which has taken place in the occult field, lest that field be abandoned to the operations of the quacks.

Now that so much has been said by both Regardie and Crowley, it is necessary to say a little more, and so elucidate the whole situation.

It must be obvious to anyone who compares them that *The Garden of Pomegranates* and *The Tree of Life*, by Regardie; *Magick*, by Crowley; and *The Mystical Qabalah*, by myself, are all dealing with the same system, and the question naturally arises, who has cribbed from which? The answer to this is very simple; the system dealt with is not the private property of any one of us, but is that which I have frequently referred to in my writings as the Western Esoteric Tradition. I have always been guarded in my references to this matter, because I took some pretty stringent initiation oaths, and I do not care for the responsibility of breaking those oaths; but, as previously noted, I have never pretended ignorance of, or misled anyone concerning matters that others have taken the responsibility of making public. I have never had a taste for priestcraft, whatever other sins as chela or guru may justly be ascribed to me. Mr. Regardie's revelation frees my hands considerably further, for it does not appear to me that there is very much he has left unsaid. I expect that the pontiffs of the mysteries will tell their neophytes that his books are inaccurate and incomplete; but I think they will find, after they have served ten years for Leah and another ten for Rachel, as I was made to do, that they are neither inaccurate nor incomplete, and a very great deal better put together than the official knowledge papers and side lectures.

Now concerning the nature of these mysterious mysteries; as I have already explained, I am wrapped up in oaths of secrecy like a cat in a fly-paper, but I do not feel that this debars me from quoting the published works of other writers. When Mrs. McGregor Mathers, in her introduction to the second edition of her husband's translation of *The Kabbalah Denudata* refers, in explicit terms, to the mystery school he founded, and intimates that admission may be obtained thereto by applying to her, care of her publishers, and when she publishes a pamphlet for propaganda purposes in the United States which is even more explicit, who am I that should plead ignorance of the existence of such an Order? And when W. B. Yeats says, in his autobiography, that the Order founded by Mr. Mathers was called the "Golden Dawn", am I to pretend that I do not know what the mysterious initials G.D. stand for? Am I also to pretend, in view of what he has to say of his experiences while he was a member, and of confirmatory remarks of George Moore in his autobiographical book, *Ave atque Vale*, that I do not know that the "Golden Dawn" concerns itself with ceremonial magic? Does my initiation oath require me to deny these matters or to profess my ignorance of them? If so, it requires me to tell lies.

The history of the "Golden Dawn" had been told at considerable length, and its credentials examined, by Aleister Crowley in his magazine, *The Equinox*, in which he gave the whole affair away after a quarrel with Mathers. Mr. Regardie refers to this publication in *The Tree of Life*, and quotes from the rituals that Crowley publishes. He is incorrect, however, in saying that Crowley did not reveal Mathers' system till after his death, for *The Equinox* began to appear in 1909, and Mathers died during the influenza epidemic which occurred towards the end of the war. He is also incorrect when he says that the "Golden Dawn" is defunct; it has broken up into various scattered units, of varying degrees of efficiency, but I know, personally, of four functioning lodges, all of which have got the full set of rites and teaching; and there are quite likely to be others of which I do not know, for people did not always take McGregor Mathers seriously when he cursed them and flung them into outer darkness, as he did pretty freely, but carried on with the system which they had found to be effectual for putting them in touch with the Secret Chiefs. After all, the test of the validity of a lodge or order is its power to initiate successfully, not its legal right to a charter, given or withheld at the personal judgment of individuals. Initiation is like vaccination; if it takes, there is an unmistakable reaction.

The "Golden Dawn" is alleged to owe its origin to the discovery by Mathers of a set of mysterious cipher manuscripts; these manuscripts exist, for I have talked with trustworthy persons who have seen them; but as they were in cipher, they were not able to bear testimony concerning their contents. In these manuscripts Mathers is supposed to have found the outline of the "Golden Dawn" rituals and the system of correspondences which is the key to its teaching, including the correct attribution of the Tarot Trumps on the Tree of Life, which enables them to be linked up with the astrological signs, a secret that students have long sought to discover. It is this system which Crowley uses in his *Equinox, 777, Book Four,* and his recently published *Magick;* which Regardie uses in both his books, and which I am using in my *Mystical Qabalah,* now appearing serially in my own magazine. We have none of us cribbed from each other, but have all drawn upon the Mathers manuscripts.

I personally drew direct, because I possess these manuscripts; but I did not take the responsibility of publishing them, or any of their contents, but worked from Crowley's *777,* as I acknowledge in my articles, using my knowledge of the Mathers manuscripts for counter-checking purposes. I may say that I found Crowley's books to be accurate. He himself does not acknowledge his sources in his recently published *Magick,* but in his *Equinox,* now out of print, he expressly declares that he is making public the "Golden Dawn" system as commanded by the Secret Chiefs. Regardie himself acknowledges his indebtedness to the published works of Mathers, Wynn Westcott and Crowley; but as Mathers and Wynn Westcott never put any of these correspondences into their published works, and Regardie could not have been in direct touch with the G.D. or he would have known it was not defunct, I conclude he has drawn his information from Crowley's A.A., which is simply the G.D. system under another name – or so it appears to me from what its founder says about it.

Thus I think we may claim to have traced out this system of correspondences and its antecedents: Crowley and I drew direct from Mathers' "Golden Dawn", and Regardie drew from Crowley's "A.A.".

The next point we have to solve in unravelling our mystery is the relationship of the different characters in this drama to each other. Crowley and Mathers quarrelled. Exactly why, I do not know; incompatibility of temperament was probably the fundamental cause, whatever the actual occasion of their break may have been. Crowley then started the publication of his magazine, *The Equinox,* which came out twice yearly for five years in England and made a fresh start in America after the war with one volume, but never got any further. These eleven volumes are highly prized by the more advanced students of occultism, and the complete set is hard to come by and commands high prices. Some of the contents, however, have been reprinted in *Magick,* together with a certain amount of new material.

In this magazine Crowley deliberately gave away all that he possessed of Mathers' secrets, including some of his rituals, and tore Mathers' character to shreds. I have never met either of the persons concerned in this dispute, but it appears to me that the abuse Crowley heaps on Mathers in the pages of his magazine is far more likely to reflect on himself than it is upon Mathers. In his criticisms of the manner in which Mathers conducted his organization he is, I think, upon surer ground, for I found exactly the same problems confronting me when I myself joined it some years after he left. Practical teaching from official sources was conspicuous by its absence, and unless one was lucky enough to have a personal friend among its members with a gift of exposition, one was left high and dry. One was put through the ceremonies, given the bare bones of the system in the knowledge lectures and a few commentaries on them called side lectures, for the most part of very inferior quality, and left to one's own devices. The glory had departed in the days when I knew the Order, for most of its original members were dead or withdrawn; it had suffered severely during the war, and was manned mainly by widows and grey-bearded ancients; and the widows of its founders were somewhat in the position of the widow of a certain famous artist when she was asked if she meant to carry on her husband's business. The cloak of Elijah did not necessarily descend on Mrs. Elishah. Nevertheless, anyone with any psychic perceptions at all could not fail to realize that there was power in the ceremonies and formulae; and anyone who made a study of them also speedily found out that in the system of correspondences taught in the G.D. they got something of inestimable value.

These correspondences which were scattered through the knowledge papers of the G.D. in inextricable confusion, for Mathers seemed to have a peculiar gift for putting his teaching in the most unassimilable form possible (perhaps due to too much reading of Rabbinal literature), were sorted out and assembled in readily available form by Crowley and published in his book *777*. This book is now out of print, but the more important of its contents are reprinted in the fourth volume of *Magick*. It is this book which I made use of for my *Mystical Qabalah*, and I imagine that Regardie also used it for his *Garden of Pomegranates*.

He has drawn very extensively upon Crowley's writings for his inspiration and information, and so much controversy has centred around the personality of that extraordinary man, that it is only fair to Mr. Regardie to quote a passage in which he explains his attitude in the matter.

He says, on page 40 of *The Tree of Life*: "It will be noted that I have quoted freely from Aleister Crowley, and it is imperative clearly to define my attitude towards this man of genius ... It is a pity, as I see it, that the public should be robbed of that superlative freshness and originality which are his, and deprived of those aspects of his teaching which are fine, ennobling and enduring, simply because of a certain proportion of his literary output which is certainly banal, petty, unimportant, and, no doubt, very reprehensible. The personalities and private lives of these individuals concern me not at all, and I do not feel disposed to discuss them."

This, in my opinion, is the right attitude to adopt in the matter. I do not think any educated person will dispute the statement that a man's literary work should be judged impartially as literature, and that his character should not weigh in the balance, either for or against. Ovid and Byron both had to leave their country for their country's good, but that does not prevent their writings being reckoned as great literature. In a hundred years' time, when the controversies concerning his personality have died down, Crowley will be recognised, quite apart from his occult work, as a great English writer of both prose and poetry. The man whose work finds inclusion in *The Oxford Book of Mystical Verse* can meet the jeers of even such an eminent critic as G. K. Chesterton on a level. Although Crowley's writings are marred by the grossest ribaldry and the foulest personal abuse, they are the works of a man of genius and a writer of magnificent English, and it is a great loss to occult literature that they are not available for the general reader. There could be no more valuable contribution to the occult movement then a collected edition of the works of this very great writer, edited and annotated by some such sympathetic hand as that of Mr. Regardie, and with the personalities cut out.

To speak any word in mitigation of the general condemnation of Crowley is a thankless task, for panic-stricken people immediately conclude that one is in league with the devil. Nevertheless, Mr. Regardie has had the courage to do this, and I should like to add my voice to his. To make use of a man's work without acknowledgment is no better than picking pockets.

As the "Golden Dawn", "The A.A." and my own "Inner Light" must appear to the uninformed observer to be more or less mixed up together, I feel it is advisable to disentangle them. The deeper issues of occultism are evidently going to come out into the open in the near future; therefore a clearing of the ground is imperative.

It may be as well to explain my own position in relation to the "Golden Dawn". I joined the southern branch of the Scottish section of it, since disbanded, in 1919, and transferred from there to the section of it of which Mrs. McGregor Mathers was the head, and which claimed the only orthodoxy. She nearly turned me out for writing *The Esoteric Philosophy of Love and Marriage,* on the grounds that I was betraying the inner teaching of the Order, but it was pointed out to her that I had not then got the degree in which that teaching was given, and I was pardoned. She suspended me for some months for writing *Sane Occultism,* and finally turned me out because certain symbols had not appeared in my aura – a perfectly unanswerable charge. However, I transferred again to yet another section of the Order, where, for the first time, I saw justice done to what is, in my opinion, a very great system, and continued my studies without interruption.

The "Fraternity of the Inner Light" was founded by me in agreement with Mrs. Mathers, to be an Outer Court to the "Golden Dawn" system. All went well at first, and I was in high favour; but presently I fell from grace; why, I never knew. No specific charges were ever made against me, save that of not having the proper symbols in my aura. Finally I was turned out without reason assigned, save the ridiculous one above. My experiences, when I persisted in using the Order system, I have related in *Psychic Self-Defence*. Unpleasant as those experiences were, the fact remains that Mrs. Mathers' rejection of me did not close the gates of the Order to me on either the outer or the inner planes.

I personally believe that the Temples of the Mysteries are not houses made with hands, but are eternal in the heavens. I no more believe McGregor Mathers' story of meeting mysterious adepts in the Bois de Boulogne than I believe Leadbeater's stories of the Masters and their marble seats. There is not only folly, but fraud, in confusing the planes, and representing that which was experienced subjectively as having actually happened in the world of matter.

I have given my life to occultism since I was a young girl, and everything I have seen and experienced, on both the inner and the outer planes, points away from any centralized human organization. I have seen the most extravagant claims made on behalf of some such Great White Lodge or Temple of the Illuminati, especially by certain American enterprises, for I refuse to call them occult orders; but I have never seen them substantiated. In fact, those who are loudest in their claims give out teaching which would disgrace a patent medicine circular. By their fruits ye shall know them, and the fruits of these self-styled adepti are bilious concoctions.

The eternal temple in the heavens, however, is another matter; and innumerable witnesses, of every age and faith, have borne witness to its existence; but they all declare that it is reached in vision, and not by any journey into the wilderness, however remote. It is to this eternal temple, and the Masters who rule therein, that I personally look for my inspiration and my authority to initiate. Whatever system I use is a means to an end and nothing more. I value tradition, however, because

I find it to possess a psychic efficacy which is lacking in original systems, however theoretically correct or aesthetically beautiful they may be.

It is my belief that Mathers got the keys to his system from the mysterious manuscripts, and that these connect up with the genuine European tradition whose symbol is the rose on the cross, and concerning which so little is known. I cannot prove this statement on the physical plane, because I have never been allowed a sight of those manuscripts or any opportunity to test the statements that are current in the Order concerning its origin; but from the psychic experiences I have had in connection with the "Golden Dawn" I have formed the above opinion, for what my opinion may be worth, and I may say that I have had a fairly wide range of experience in practical occultism.

It seems to me that whoever can work the system of the "Golden Dawn" in such a manner as to pick up the contacts of the Secret Chiefs need not pay very much attention to the "Trespassers will be prosecuted" boards put up on the physical plane by persons who are not altogether disinterested. The system, when worked by competent persons, is effectual, whether they are chartered or not. But even the "Golden Dawn" system, when worked by incompetent persons, is ineffectual, as I know to my cost.

It is not advisable, however, for persons with no experience of practical occultism to make their first experiments with no other guidance than that of a book. Preliminary training is necessary; also a guide with a rope in case of difficulties. But those who have already passed through the Outer Court and stand waiting at the Door Between the Pylons will find, in Mr. Regardie's books, the keys they need. I, for one, wish them Godspeed on their journey; and may they find the Stone of the wise; the *Summum Bonum;* true wisdom; perfect happiness.

The Occult Review, January 1933

~⊙ Appendix 2 ⊙~
THE NOVELS OF DION FORTUNE

By DION FORTUNE

Article by Dion Fortune in "The Inner Light Magazine", 1936

To write a review of one's own books is not easy, and to find a suitable title for that review is even more difficult. Therefore a plain and straightforward statement of fact may be the simplest solution of the problem for both title and review, and in the end serve more effectually the purpose I have in mind than any more elaborate process might do.

Let me first of all answer a question which is not infrequently being asked. People say: "We like your *Mystical Qabalah*, or your *Meditations on the Collects* (according to the taste and type of correspondent), but why do you waste your time writing occult thrillers?" It has even been complained by a well-known authority that the language I put into the mouths of my characters is that of a fourth form schoolboy, and that mystic literature cannot be written on these lines.

To this I reply that I write my occult stories in the form of 'thrillers' because I am by temperament and training a journalist and fiction writer, and to write them otherwise would be to me incompetent craftsmanship; and when I see what other folk, who have never endured the discipline of the blue pencil, produce in the way of mystic parables, I am entirely unrepentant.

My novels are quite definitely 'stories with a purpose'; but I equally definitely decline to subordinate the story to the purpose, for that, I consider, is the trade-mark of technical incompetence; moreover, it defeats its own end.

It may also be alleged against me that a story with a purpose is a literary hermaphrodite incapable of function either way, and that the purpose would fare better in plain prose. To this I reply that every story worthy of the name is a story with a purpose; it must have its roots in some basic idea if it is not to be merely episodic, and the difference between the work of a creative writer and a literary hack lies in the very fact that his stories have germinated like seed from the soil of a basic idea, instead of being put together like paper flowers on an unattached stalk for display and nothing more.

I have finally to answer the charge of using, upon occasion, the language of Smith Minor in reference to the eternal verities of the soul.

Personally I had thought that Dr Johnson was as dead as his patroness, Queen Anne, and that the stilted language of the toddlers in *The Fairchild Family* was only reproduced nowadays in such books as *The Young Visitors*, and that to have me brought up on this charge was rather like a prosecution for Sabbath-breaking under the Vagrancy Acts of Queen Elizabeth.

The answer to these three charges is to be sought in the purpose and method of my novel-writing as a whole. Let me therefore explain what I am about in these novels, and why I do it.

The first reason that I write novels, and perhaps the best possible reason, is that I am a novel-writer; that is to say, I have the story-teller's imagination, and *must* write novels, whether they serve any useful purpose or not, in the same way that a hen must lay eggs, for otherwise the poor creature would burst.[7] But because I have a purpose in my life, which is the work of initiation organised as The Fraternity of the Inner Light, my novels have a purpose, which is the purpose of initiation. Therefore my novels have not got a purpose stuck on like a luggage label, after the dreadful manner of the allegorists, but spring from my purpose as the seed from the soil in which it germinates, into which it strikes its roots, and from which it draws it vitality.

Allowing therefore for the fact that I would write novels anyway, even if I did not write occult novels, let me explain why I consider the occult novels an important part of the work that is being done by means of The Fraternity of the Inner Light.

In the first place, these novels are read by people through the

---

7 She also wrote a series of thriller-romances under the pen-name of V.M.Steele: *The Scarred Wrists; Hunters of Humans; Beloved of Ishmael* (Stanley Paul 1935, 1935, 1936) & *The Yellow Shadow* (Quality Press, 1942). They have no esoteric content.

circulating libraries who would not sit down to read a prose work on occultism; and of the people who read my books as 'thrillers' and nothing more, there are a scattered few who see below the surface, recognise that there is something more in them that 'thrills', and receive their first awakening from their pages.

But these books are not mere propaganda; if they were, something much more saccharine and sanguinary would serve the purpose better; they are – quite unintentionally in the first instance – closely akin to the initiation dramas of the ancient Mysteries in that they take the reader by way of dramatic representations to a realisation of the nature of the soul. They are the poor relations of such writings as *The Golden Ass* of Apuleius, and The Sixth Book of the *Aeneid*.

This, of course, comes out more clearly in the later books, which are constructed to a definite pattern based upon the Qabalistic Tree of Life. *The Secrets of Dr Taverner* had a purpose that lay very near the surface – it was written to point out the possibilities that lay in the application to psychotherapy of the knowledge to be found in occult science, and said so frankly in the foreword.

The Demon Lover set out to be a thriller pure and simple, but developed a purpose spontaneously in the course of its writing – and ended up as a kind of saga of the purification of the soul through initiation; pointing out that once that process is set going, it will work itself out whether the neophyte likes it or not.

These two stand apart as early work, written a dozen years ago; then come all the prose works that established the "Inner Light" as an organised system of teaching; and then follows a trilogy, which will, I hope, expand into a decameron, given time and appreciation. The first of these, *The Winged Bull* was published last year with results that were to be expected – the reviewers passed by on the other side; a fair number of folk wrote to express unbridled admiration; and a few let off screeches of agony and abuse which showed that their complexes had been trodden on. In fact our library is enriched by a copy which was presented by a lady who was so horrified at it that she not only would not keep it in the house, but would not place it in the dustbin lest it corrupt the scavengers. This copy was in good condition and showed no signs of having been thrown across the room as stated, but from the state of the binding it was plain that it had been read from cover to cover.

The second of these, *The Goat-Foot God,* will be out soon after these pages appear in print; and the third, *The Sea Priestess,* will, I hope, come out in the spring, or at latest, the following autumn.

Now these three, though there is nothing in their plots to connect them and they are in no sense sequels of each other, must be considered as parts of a coherent whole; therefore I must speak of the unpublished as well as the published ones in order to make comprehensible what I have to say. In order to understand these novels it must be realised that each one springs from a basic idea; it is a thesis in dramatic form. In that case, then, it may be asked why I do not write it in the form of a thesis? Could I not make my point much more clearly this way than presenting it thus in a glass darkly? To answer this question I must indulge in a digression into psychology, and especially the psychology of the subconscious mind with all its complexes and dissociations.

I do not think there is any doubt that the foundation upon which the whole of my work is built is the training I had in psychoanalysis. During the three years that I spent working at a clinic for nervous diseases I got a great insight into the nature of the mind, and also into the nature and extent of the problems of life that give rise to its functional disorders. But equally I saw that although psychoanalysis could diagnose, it had no real remedy to offer, and in actual practice did not get results. It was in the quest for a solution to the problems of life and its pathologies that I came in touch with occultism, and found that the two methods, psychology and occultism, with their practical applications in psychoanalysis and initiation, fitted each other like key and lock. From this realisation everything else that I have done has followed.

In my earlier books I was engaged in interpreting occultism in the light of psychology; but in my novels I have begun to interpret psychology in the light of occultism, and I chose the form of fiction for certain very definite reasons.

In the first place, as those who know both psychoanalysis and occultism will be aware, I was bringing saltpetre and sulphur together; for psychology throws so much light on occultism that it lays bare the secrets of the inner chamber. To present these to the uninitiated is fair neither to the secrets nor to the uninitiated, as is witnessed by the reaction of the lady who feared the effect of my book on her ashbin.

On the other hand, there are a surprisingly large number of people in the world today who, though they have never seen the inside of a lodge, are of an advanced grade of enlightenment; and owing to the deservedly ill repute into which occultism has fallen owing to the knavery of some and the foolery of others, will have nothing to do with it. To these, and especially to those in whom the realisation is subconscious rather than conscious, as is often the case, a book such as my *Winged Bull* can have all the effect of an initiation because it speaks directly to the subconscious by the method of imagery, which is the only language the subconscious understands. *The Winged Bull*, in fact, together with its two companions, is an initiation drama.

Now let us make another digression and consider the psychology of the initiation drama. In the dramatic type of initiation the initiate is made to identify himself with the sufferings, death, and resurrection of some semi-divine person or avatar of a god. By this means he is given a profound emotional experience, effectual in proportion to his powers of imagination and his sympathy with the divine character portrayed.

The readers of fiction, on the other hand, can be divided into two types – those who read for intellectual pleasure, and those who read in order to escape from reality into the world of wish-fulfilment. The writers who cater for these two classes are correspondingly of two types; for the former are the classical writers, such as Thomas Hardy, Meredith, Tolstoy, Balzac, Henry James, and many more. Theirs is the literature of interpretation. They present life as an artistic composition, and their mode of presentation is their commentary on it.

To the second class belong those writers who produce thrillers and romances – such as *The Sheik*, *Tarzan of the Apes* and *The Law of the Lariat*. They represent a world that never did exist; never could exist, and would be a farcical nightmare if by any abrogation of natural law it came into being. But they have an enormous appeal because they speak to the subconscious minds of an enormous number of people and answer to their subconscious needs.

For they offer a way of escape from the monotonous limitations of life as it is lived on a limited income, or by a limited soul whatever the income. Very few readers read a book objectively, as a spectator and nothing more; they tend, in varying degree according to their type and the type of the book, to live in it imaginatively, and if the type is congenial, to identify themselves with the hero or the heroine as the case may be, and so the book becomes a glorified day-dream; and where there is any imaginative power in the mind, the plot of the book is carried on into actual day-dreaming, and where the imaginative power of the mind is sufficiently great, even into the dreams of sleep. In fact, when a psychoanalysis is being carried out, it is invariably found that an enormous amount of the material is drawn from the books recently read.

We have, then, the two types of novels – the novels of interpretation, and the novels of wish-fulfilment. Knowing this as a novelist, and also knowing as a psychologist the part played by the day-dream, I decided to put the two together and produce novels that should come as near an initiation ceremony as possible; that is to say, that should produce in receptive persons something of the same results as produced by the experience of going through a ritual initiation.

Now a ritual initiation, if it is to be anything save a pious farce, must bear a definite relationship to life; it should represent a stage in the unfoldment of the higher self. It is a well-known saying in the Mystery Tradition that life is the Great Initiator; and so it is. But life initiates very slowly, and very painfully, and much time is wasted in groping in darkness for want of a guide. Life will initiate in the same way as the weather will wear down a mountain range by erosion. The adept is like the engineer who comes along and blasts the rock and makes a graded way through the range.

In writing my novels I used exactly the same method that is used in the composition of a ritual. But, my readers may say, we have always understood that the rituals are traditional, and of great antiquity. This is perfectly true; there are traditional rituals, of which one would not change one jot or one tittle lest one impaired their efficacy; but a practising occultist is constantly making his own rituals for whatever purpose he may have in hand; in fact it is one of the tests of a properly trained initiate that he can make a ritual for a given purpose, and that it will produce results. There are certain principles of ritual-making which are so well known as to be standardised within the Mystery Tradition, and every initiate worthy of the name is familiar with these. A great deal of secrecy has been observed with regard to them, though they are scattered through innumerable published works and unpublished papers. Finally, I have gathered them all together and published the essence of them in my *Mystical Qabalah*. Those who know that book will see that my novels are Qabalistic works.

In each case I have taken a basic idea, attributed it to its appropriate Sephirah in the proper Qabalistic manner, and then proceeded to work it out on the basis, not of Qabalistic symbolism as I should have done if I were writing an occult treatise on the subject, but of the dream-symbolism of psychoanalysis. Consequently, anyone who knows psychoanalysis can take these novels to pieces as if they were dreams, and anyone who knows the Qabalah can 'place them on the Tree'.

Now the peculiar function of the famous Tree of Life of the Qabalists is to link the microcosm with the macrocosm; in other words, to reveal the relationship between the different factors in the soul of man and the corresponding factors in the cosmic life from which they derive, causing a tremendous inflow of energy and inspiration into the aspect of the soul thus linked with its cosmic prototype; gods, elemental kings and *hoc genus omne*; actually these Great Ones are the projections and dramatisations of the factors that go to the make-up of the human soul; but equally they are something much more than that, according to occult tradition, reinforced by modern experience; they are the channels of the corresponding spiritual forces owing to the faculty of the mind for being energised by an idea.

Now supposing we get a novel that is at the same time an interpretation and a day-dream, have we not got something very potent; especially if that interpretation be a mystical and cosmic one? This is precisely what I have tried to do with my novels. I have tried to make use of the dramatic form of the thriller-romance, as a vehicle for a mystical and cosmic interpretation. Read by a person who has it in him to respond, these stories will put him in touch with the corresponding cosmic factor through his day-dream identification of himself with the hero who is put in touch with cosmic factors in the course of the story; in fact each story is the story of an initiation, and if the reader identifies himself with the hero, or herself with the heroine, they will be taken through that initiation as surely as a young sporting dog is trained to be coupled to an obedient and gun-wise beast who knows the words of command.

If, of course, there is no capacity for response, the reader will probably classify the stories with *Tarzan of the Apes*. If there is a capacity for response, and at the same time repressions and dissociations or the particular type of psychopathology corresponding to the thesis of the book, the reader will, I am afraid, 'go off the deep end', as witness the lady of the ashbin. They will have the equivalent of a fairly severe psychic shock because the book has spoken to their subconsciousness words they do not desire to hear. Incidentally, they will probably accuse me of all the sins of the Decalogue, and all the crimes in the Newgate calendar because these represent the infantile repressions which have been stirred within them; and they will do it with a vehemence, with a degree of emotion, with even an intensity of fear which will leave no one who knows any psychology in any doubt as to what has happened or which complex has been trodden on. One of these days I may be lucky enough to be reviewed by a reviewer with a complex, and then my fortune is made! It is an interesting fact that wherever in the pages of my books the symbolism is working down onto the deeper levels of the mind, there is always a phenomenal crop of printer's errors in the proofs.

I may, perhaps, add that at the time I wrote my novels I had not come across Nietzsche's *Birth of Tragedy*, and that when I read it, it was just as much a revelation to me as I had hoped that my stories would be to other readers; for in those rather difficult pages I found analysed in terms of aesthetics and metaphysics exactly what I had been trying to do in my fiction.

I must apologise for a digression into autobiography, but its purpose is to explain that a hard and exacting discipline, first of quality and then of quantity, had furnished me with a literary style that was an absolutely pliable tool in my hand; rapid, effortless, requiring the minimum of revision, so that the first draft can generally go to the printers uncopied. In fact, constant unceasing paper-covering resulted in a facility that allowed of my subconscious getting itself down on paper. Consequently my novels are dramatised day-dreams. They are not written; they are lived and recorded. Everything is seen and heard exactly as if I were watching a play at the theatre.

Those who are acquainted with the theory and practice of magic, especially as outlined in *The Mystical Qabalah* and in various recent articles in these pages, will know that vividly visualised thought-forms become astral images, ensouled by cosmic forces – provided they are built upon cosmic lines – nothing, for instance, could vivify a hippogriff. Now my characters are human beings; even the reviewers who like them least have always granted me that. Consequently my books, so far as I can judge of my own work, appear to me to 'come alive' in a peculiar way. They are, in fact, magical acts.

Point by point I am taking the great problems of human life as I conceive them; analysing them in the experiences of my characters; explaining them in their speeches – for the books are full of apparently random comments scattered through the pages as the plot goes on; and finding the ultimate happy ending in a definite, practical, psycho-magical solution, and showing exactly how it was done, so that anybody with a similar problem can go and do likewise. These books are, in fact, psychotherapy; each one is both an initiation to a particular Sephirah and a psychoanalysis according to the capacity for response of the reader.

~ Appendix 3 ~

THE WINGED BULL:
A STUDY IN ESOTERIC PSYCHOLOGY

By DION FORTUNE

Article by Dion Fortune in "The Inner Light Magazine", 1938

THE message that the Fraternity of the Inner Light has to give is not one that is easily put into words. Traditionally, esoteric teaching is only conveyed by glyph and symbol and dramatic ritual. In an earlier stage of human development, and among races today whose minds are still at that early stage of development, this graphic and concrete method of presentation was well understood, for indeed their minds worked in no other way; but today, among civilised people, all the higher thinking is done in words, not in pictures in the imagination, and symbolic presentation too often misses its mark. The average man does not know how to approach it, or how to make use of it, and certain tracts of the mind are in consequence closed to him. This is a great loss, for those tracts contain Golconda and the mines of Ophir.

In an attempt to compromise between the symbolic and the rational methods of presentation I decided to avail myself of the form of fiction as being a mode of presentation which could approach the subconscious levels of the mind, which think in images, without losing touch with the conscious levels of the mind which think in words, thus making contact once again with those potent levels of the mind that have fallen into disuse in modern civilisation.

The result of this experiment has been interesting. The novels have quite definitely spoken to the subconsciousness of their readers, exercising over some a curious and profound fascination, and throwing others into something not far removed from panic as they felt the stirring of the depths. They have failed in a large measure, however, to accomplish their main object, which was the linking up of consciousness and subconsciousness, bringing both to bear simultaneously upon certain things, and also bringing them to bear upon each other. In order to remove this difficulty I propose to 'take the works to pieces', and show what I have been trying to do, and how I have done it. With this end in view, I will make a detailed analysis of *The Winged Bull*, the first of the trilogy, which serves as a general introduction to the other two, and, for the matter of that, to any books that may come after them; for these novels are neither pot-boilers or romances, but essays in applied psychology, and the psychology is applied first and foremost to the reader.

The Winged Bull, which came first and was something of an experiment, contains three basic ideas interacting with each other to supply the motive and form the element of conflict in a story, without which no plot is possible. This makes it more difficult to analyse, and therefore more in need of analysis, than its two companions, which are each built around the nucleus of a single idea.

The key-concept of *The Winged Bull*, in which the three basic motifs are subsumed, is frankly stated in the 'blurb' – "the relationship between a man and a woman in the light of the forgotten knowledge of the ancients", and concerns "the knowledge of certain aspects of the sex relationship which are the carefully guarded secrets of the initiates". That they are carefully guarded is proven by the fact that Mrs McGregor Mathers nearly turned me out of the famous Fraternity of the Golden Dawn, in which I received a part of my training, for touching upon the mere fringe of them in an earlier book of mine, *The Esoteric Philosophy of Love and Marriage*.

These are things that it is not easy to put down flatly in black and white; they are liable to be misunderstood, or understood and abused. The form of fiction was used in order that those who had problems that could be solved by this knowledge might find that these stories 'spoke to their condition'. This has proved to be the case. Those whom life had initiated were quickly onto the significance of these books, but unless they were already well-versed not only in occult studies, but also in analytical psychology, they were not able to make the necessary practical applications of the doctrine and so straighten themselves out; hence the necessity for more explicit explanation.

No doubt these explanations will be pitched on by many people as indicating that the Fraternity of the Inner Light is concerned with all manner of unimaginable evil, all the more evil for being unimaginable. To this I reply by asking any critics who may come forward, to open the argument by defining what they understand by evil, and we will then be in a position to decide whether that definition applies to my books or not.

I am not sufficiently well versed to be able to express an opinion upon the conditions prevailing in countries other than my own and the United States, but it is hardly possible to deny that marriage in countries adhering to Anglo-Saxon ideals is in a pretty bad way, and that its stock is quoted low on a falling market. The evidence for this is to be found in three separate quarters; firstly in the divorce statistics; secondly in the clinics for functional nervous disorders; and thirdly in the rising tide of loose living and promiscuity which is rapidly reaching flood level. Something is very much wrong, and it will not be remedied by stiffening the divorce laws or the Criminal Law Amendment Act: to cope with it by psychotherapy alone, valuable as this can be, is like nursing the victims of a typhoid epidemic and leaving the contaminated water supply undealt with.

No one who has taken the trouble to inform themselves at all adequately concerning the facts of life can be unaware that the conventional attitude towards these facts is on a par with the early Victorian attitude towards dietetics, which produced gout, anaemia and rickets in such quantities that they came to be looked upon as the normal accompaniments of civilised life.

There have been many races known to history that have become extinct, not because they were conquered in war, or because of changes of climate in their habitat, but because they persistently practised irrational and unhygienic customs, usually from religious motives. Others, notably the Jews, have survived and retained their racial purity under most adverse conditions because their social customs were notably hygienic. The kind of customs that have been followed by heathen peoples under the belief that they were pleasing to their gods, or essential to holiness, are so amazing, so irrational, and so cruel as to be not only unbelievable, but unimaginable by civilised minds. Those who wish to follow up the subject will find the material set forth authoritatively by that great scholar, Sir James Frazer in his classic work *The Golden Bough* and notably in the two volumes entitled *Attis, Adonis and Osiris*. Much additional material of great interest and immediate bearing on modern problems is also to be found in the three volumes of Briffault's monumental work entitled *The Mothers*. A shorter, but very valuable work, in which the psychological inferences are drawn from this mass of ethnological date, is Dr Brand's *Sacrifice to Attis*.

Human nature itself varies very little, historically or geographically; the variations that produce its infinite superficial variety are to be sought in education and environment: consequently there is a great deal we can learn from the experiences of primitive peoples, or people with different types of civilisation to our own, if we choose to make the obvious application. Observing the crippling effect upon the South Sea Islanders of their absurd system of taboos, or upon the Hindus of their cruel and baseless caste prejudices; or of the very widespread totem system, which causes whole tribes to suffer from malnutrition because certain types of wholesome and abundant food are forbidden to them from superstitious motives, shall we follow the example of the Pharisee and thank God that we are not as other men, or shall we face the issue frankly and ask ourselves whether we and our sacred civilisation are immune from the universal human disease of projecting our subconscious fears as bogies and then worshipping them, and whether some of our most cherished, most firmly established, most fundamental ideas may not furnish subject matter for the ethnologists of the future; whether, if looked at impartially, conventional morality is not as cruel in its operation as anything the South Sea Islanders have produced, and what passes for social hygiene among uplift organisations as ignorant and unhygienic as the worst efforts of totem and taboo?

One has only to see, as I have seen, the steady stream of cases going through a psychological clinic, to know that this is the fact, for the vast majority of these cases are due simply and solely to our unhygienic social system.

The trouble is due, in the first place, to the fact that Christianity took its ethics, not from the sanity of Moses, but from the unbalanced mentality of St Augustine. To see how unbalanced that mentality was, one has only to read his *Confessions* in the light of a modicum of psychological knowledge. He was a rake with a strong mother fixation, which Monica exploited for all she was worth. The result was a terrific psychological conflict which was finally resolved in conversion, and compensated, and over-compensated, in asceticism. A very large proportion of the social ills that have haunted Christendom through its history are attributable to the fact that its morality bears the stamp, not of a balanced mind such as that of Moses or the Buddha, but of the cranky mind of Monica's neurotic son.

Those who came after him followed in his footsteps, and the history of the saints reads like a treatise on psycho-pathology; it is, in fact, a horrifying chronicle of sick minds and sick bodies. Let those who doubt this statement go to the original sources and read for themselves. Do not let them be contented with *The Little Flowers of St Francis* or *The Little Plays of St Francis*, but go to the actual history, compiled from the writings of the saint and his companions, and see the amazing background of filth and folly that has been smoothed away and covered up for the benefit of modern readers; and, in the light of what they will learn from historical sources, ask themselves whether what came out at the recent trials of several hundred Franciscan monks in Germany is altogether surprising.[8] But even if these unhappy men were justly convicted of the unmentionable offences for which they were put on trial, and any one who has seen the faces in the ranks of a seminary out for a walk would be little inclined to risk giving them the benefit of the doubt, does it follow that they were justly punished for them? May it not be that a system that has so consistently given rise to these troubles should itself be put on trial?

The recorded teachings of Jesus on the subject of sexual morality are too scanty to be made into a working system; consequently, Christian sexual morality is the least Christian thing about Christendom. It is the work, not of Our Lord, nor of the disciples, nor even of the apostles, but of the Early Fathers and successive Church Councils, and in the opinion of any impartial observer of the results obtained, they have botched their work exceedingly badly. We have a standard of living for normal people based upon the counsels of saints and ascetics. It

---

8   Trial in Rhineland town of Waldbreitbach in 1936 of 276 Franciscan monks for various sexual offences, including paedophilia – although not without elements of a Nazi political show trial.

just doesn't work; and just as the railway men only run the trains on time by ignoring all manner of 'Safety First' regulations, so human life is only rendered liveable by a series of compromises, hypocrisies, evasions, and sheer law-breaking. Any one who doubts this need only turn to the marriage service in the prayer book, wherein it is stated in the plainest possible language that marriage is grudgingly tolerated as a remedy for sin: that Christianity, having failed to stamp out sex life is reluctantly obliged to regulate it in order to minimise its evils as far as possible: that it is tolerated from necessity, not choice, and then only within the narrowest possible limits.

The history both of society and medicine has proved this policy to have been universally disastrous. We have built up a system of taboos in no way differing from those of the South Sea Islanders, and we have borne the same burden of purposeless and needless suffering that we deplore in their case and seek to remedy by a more enlightened teaching. Of recent years pioneers, of whom Havelock Ellis and Freud are the most notable, have tried to do for Europeans what missionaries are doing for the Polynesians, and with much the same results. It is true that these two courageous men have not been actually killed and eaten, but the spirit of cannibalism has in no wise been lacking in our midst.

They have broken down the Great Taboo in much the same way as musk-rats break down a dam – they drive their relatively minute tunnels here and there, and the pressure of the water does the rest. People have started to think, talk and read on the subject of social hygiene, and the Great Taboo is melting away like a flooded dyke.

This changed state of affairs, however, is contributing nearly as many evils to the problem of human life as the regime it is replacing. It is a very demoralising thing to be called upon to work an unworkable system, because the unavoidable compromises and evasions undermine personal morale even while they serve the very necessary purpose of holding the social structure together: but harmful as it is, it is less harmful than having no system at all. Any sort of centralised control is better than a complete breakdown of organisation; however incompetent, however venal, it staves off the worst results of disintegration. There are people who say that no reconstruction is possible until the ground has been cleared, and it is better to let an inherent unsound system collapse, or even to push it over, than to prolong the agony of patching it up.

Now this may be in the case of inanimate objects such as obsolete house property, but if you have no option but to conduct 'business as usual during the alterations to the premises', you are exceedingly unwise to conduct those alterations with dynamite. You must do as the great contractors do – underpinning, buttressing, pulling out a girder at a time and replacing it, and generally keeping the whole building weather-tight and inhabitable while the operation is going on.

It is as a contribution to the rebuilding operations that my three novels were written. It is a simple enough operation to make a clean sweep of existing problems, in fiction at any rate, as H.G. Wells has done, and propound a perfect scheme for the perfect future, provided, of course, you can be sure of getting perfect human nature to operate it. It is easy enough to expose human foibles and follies as Bernard Shaw has done, or display them as Aldous Huxley does. It is of great interest, and some value to analyse human life psychologically as May Sinclair has done, but at the end of it all, where are we? Has any one a workable scheme to put forward? A scheme that shall be workable at the present moment, in a transition age, and does not require the Millennium for its inception?

May Sinclair used to come to the psychological clinic at which I worked. She attended the lectures there, and then wrote her psychological novels; but she did not see the routine work of the treatment rooms, nor the records of the follow-up files. Those are a very different story to the stories of fiction. I have seen a great deal of the inside workings of psychotherapy, and if the truth were told, it would have to be admitted that it is the least promising branch of therapeutics, even less promising than cancer research, which is saying a good deal. Both these branches of research have made valuable contributions to our diagnostic knowledge, but their contributions to therapeutics are considerably less extensive. In plain English, they have improved the supply of labels, and that is about all.

In psychotherapy enough is known of the nature of the mind to enable useful advice to be given to the patient; but if the patient cannot take it owing to his circumstances, or will not take it owing to the disorganising effect of his disease, there is very little the psychotherapist can do for him. Occupational therapy, therapeutic conversation, psycho-analysis, suggestion and hypnosis are about all he has to offer. It is as if a physician had to face all eventualities with a bottle of aspirin in one hand and of jalap in the other. The one is a very mild sedative, and the other a most disruptive agent of purification.

The only really effective method of handling the mind is the method used by the occultists, but they are under the delusion that they are dealing with angels, archangels, principalities and powers, and are, for the most part, entirely lacking in that which is the sole virtue of modern psychology, its diagnostic capacity. The occultist is like a man with a can of petrol and a box of matches; the psycho-therapist the driver of a car with an empty tank. If they could be brought together, results would follow. If the petrol merchant is allowed to strike matches, results will also follow, but not, perhaps, those intended.

The Winged Bull has for its threefold thesis firstly, the radical unsoundness of the Christian attitude towards sex; secondly, the remedial possibilities of a combination of psychology and occultism; thirdly, the dangers of the black side of sexual magic. A great deal more could be said on this latter subject than was said in the pages of *The Winged Bull*, which were, however, as plain-spoken as I thought the form of fiction would stand. In addition to this, the book moves against a background of all the odd erudition, if erudition it can be called, that has accumulated in my mind during twenty years of occult work. There is nothing in it that is fanciful or far-fetched, not even the most passing of *obiter dicta*, but for all the innumerable odds and ends of information the book contains, chapter and verse could be given from recognised sources or personal experience.

The amount of information there is in that book amazed even me when I came to read it. For speaking to the subconscious as it does, it likewise speaks from the subconscious; and my subconscious, as all subconsciousnesses must, contains a great deal more than I realised was there till it rose to the surface in the course of the writing.

To appreciate what follows it is necessary to be familiar with the book, and this familiarity I propose to take for granted, no epitome of the plot being of any real value. There are five main characters in the book: Brangwyn, Murchison, Astley, Frank Fouldes, and Ursula Brangwyn: the rest are stage properties. From the interaction of the temperaments of these five persons the plot works out; there is no arbitrary plot of events apart from the interplay of character; but their characters being what they are, they give rise to plenty of incident.

The role of Brangwyn is that of Greek chorus; he is the man of knowledge whose comments explain the inner working of the action. He plays less and less part as the book goes on because less and less comment is needed as action develops out of the pre-explained bases. This is a weakness in the structure of the book but an actuality in the psychology, for he would naturally and inevitably recede into the background as Murchison, whom he had instructed, took up the running.

It has often been complained of my books that my characters are not altogether estimable. There are apparently, people still left alive who like to hiss the villain after the good old standards of Surrey-side melodrama. But alas, human nature is not altogether estimable, and whatever my characters may or may not be, they are at least human beings. Brangwyn, who ought, being represented as an adept, to be likewise a plaster saint – according to my critics, anyway, which shows how much they know about adepts – is represented as a man, who, although he has great knowledge, is not perfect in wisdom. This, they say, is a weakness in the book, overlooking the fact that if Brangwyn had been perfect in wisdom, there would have been no plot, because he would have nipped Fouldes in the bud and Ursula would never have got involved with him.

Is this true to the psychology of an adept? I only know that it is true to my psychology; and the psychology of Mme Blavatsky and Mrs Besant, though whether any or all of us are adepts is a matter of taste. The explanation is simple. An adept is, *ipso facto*, a psychic, and therefore sensitive. Being sensitive, he is highly suggestible. As long as he maintains the guru-chela attitude, with the chela sitting safely at his feet, he is all right, for the chela is negative and receptive towards him, and this makes him positive towards the chela; but the moment he meets the children of this world on a level, he is at their mercy. It is for this reason that I never deal directly with any save my senior students, but always through the intermediary of persons more worldly-wise and less sensitive than myself. Brangwyn made the mistake of seeing only the good in Fouldes and overlooking the weaknesses, because when with him, Fouldes was always his best self; Brangwyn did not see his worst self because, temporarily, it was non-existent. While under the immediate influence of Brangwyn Fouldes was, for the time being, the man Brangwyn wanted him to be. But when the novelty wore off, his true nature reasserted itself, and Brangwyn was let in for trouble. One may well say that Brangwyn was lacking in shrewdness for not seeing what was latent in Fouldes, yet, when Fouldes was under his influence, it was not there to be seen. It is in this manner that the adept develops his pupils; he calls out the higher self and makes it function: it is done quite unconsciously on his part, not by what he *does*, but by what he *is*. If the foundations of character are too insecure to stand the strain, the pupil slips onto the Left-hand Path, and that is bad karma for teacher as well as pupil. Note however that the reason that Fouldes went to the bad was the same reason that Brangwyn made an error of judgment in regard to him – the hyper-suggestibility of the psychic, which laid him open to the influence of Astley. Brangwyn, however, although he was not worldly-wise enough to discern the latent weakness of Fouldes, was very well able to gauge his rate of progress on the Path, and withhold the deeper teaching until he was ready for it; it was this that really incensed Fouldes and sent him off to investigate Astley, and from that act of disloyalty to the White Master came the power over him of the Dark Master.

The drawing of characters in fiction is a highly magical act. There is a definite life and vitality about true creations, and their author cannot do as he likes with them, for they have a will of their own. Many authors have confessed to this; in fact Eden Philpotts has even said that he never knows how the plot is going to work out when he starts a book, but having created his characters and placed them in the opening situation, he leaves the working out of the plot to them. For myself, I am very much the spectator in my novels, looking through into the world in which my characters move as if gazing in at a lit window after dark. So definite is this sense of reality that if I visualise a house or landscape as arranged in a particular way, I am powerless to change it afterwards, and all the action of the plot has to be adapted to it. If, for instance, the plot subsequently demands that a door shall be on the north side of a house instead of the south, it is no more in my power to rearrange that house without destroying the sense of reality than it would be to shift the door if it were in actual bricks and mortar, and the characters have got to run round the house as best they can, for if I destroy the sense of reality, all creative power dries up and the task of writing comes to a standstill.

I do not draw my characters from individuals, but I definitely draw them from life, taking here a trait and there a characteristic, all of the most fragmentary. From some trait that catches my eye, I build up all the rest. It is, as Kipling says of certain Irregulars of the Boer War: "Begging the loan of a head-stall and fitting a horse to the same." Ursula Brangwyn, for instance, is built up on the nucleus of a girl seen dancing at a ball: of her I know nothing whatever beyond the way she carried her head. Murchison is built up on the nucleus of the chance-met friend of a friend in the Park, who aired his grievances on post-war conditions. Though he had done well in the War, there was no place for him in civil life, and it was not difficult to see why. And so with each of the characters, right down to Gwennie; each is built up on a nucleus of actual reality and therefore is real. All the same, I do not think any of my friends have cause to complain that I have committed the unpardonable vulgarity of pillorying them. As for the exposé of the methods of black magic in those pages, it is difficult to give an account of actual happenings without someone recognising the original; I have therefore painted a composite portrait and a composite landscape.

Oddly enough, in every character there is always a bit of myself, men as well as women; and even more oddly, there is often more of me in the men than in the women. For instance, there is very little of me in Ursula Brangwyn; only, I think, the quality of mind that is given by being trained by a man. As Murchison said of her, she is a "long, narrow strip of swank, not my style at all." In Brangwyn there is a very great deal of me, and not a little even in the unsavoury Astley. How often have I lent a hand at just such carpentering as he did! I would, however, have cleaned the billy-goat out more regularly. My first teacher was a decidedly Isabella-coloured individual, and he had just such a hugger-mugger household as Astley's. It is a curious fact that if anything goes wrong on the Inner Planes, people seem incapable of keeping their mundane affairs in any sort of order: debts and dirt accumulate at a pace unknown among ordinary mortals.

Personally, I think it is the bit of myself which is invariably included that gives the vitality to my characters. As I said before, the creation of characters in fiction is a highly magical process. The prototype of 'Dr Taverner' was the best side of my original teacher; it is an odd fact that when the stories came out in serial form in the *Royal Magazine*, the illustrator produced a most excellent likeness of that man, though he had neither description nor picture of him, nor had seen either him or me. He drew the likeness simply from his imagination after reading the stories, and it was a speaking likeness.

The scenes of *The Winged Bull* are five in number, and none of them are chosen at random, but because they are the appropriate background of the action that takes place there. Anyone who is at all sensitive knows that places have very definite psychic characteristics, and these characteristics are exploited to the full in this story.

The main movement of the plot is in Bloomsbury. Now why Bloomsbury? Because it is a peculiarly potent spot psychically. Why this should be, I do not know. Perhaps its cosmopolitan population has something to do with it, being more free from repression than the average Anglo-Saxon. Perhaps the Old Gods housed in the British Museum play a part. Moreover, it is rumoured that the Black Mass is worked regularly in a turning off the Tottenham Court Road. Be that as it may, Bloomsbury is a district in which it is easy to do magic, and so is Chelsea; whereas in the neighbouring Fulham it is very up-hill work. With Bloomsbury, where Brangwyn lives, is contrasted Acton, where Murchison's clerical brother lives and has the unfortunate Ted as an unwilling lodger. I have no grudge against Acton, nor any associations with it, save that I once sent my clothes to a laundry there that tore them to bits; but the deadness of suburban life had to be contrasted with the liveliness of the rather raffish Bohemia of Bloomsbury, and the scanty association of the destructive laundry served to decide which suburb should bear the odium.

The choice of Snowdonia for Brangwyn's hermitage was determined by the fact that the prototype of Ursula Brangwyn was seen at a Welsh Rugger ball, and was probably of Welsh extraction; consequently the power centre where Brangwyn would make his retreat would be a Keltic one. If a line is drawn from St Alban's Head in Dorset to Lindisfarne off the coast of Northumberland, all the Keltic contacts are found on one side of it, and all the Norse contacts on the other. The Keltic Ursula is contrasted with the Norse Murchison, and on this turns much of the inner magic of the book, as will be appreciated by advanced students of these subjects, but as is not explicitly stated in the pages of the novel. Between them, they held both lines of contact that are available in these islands. Contact is a matter of both race and racial tradition, and only those who are of high grade can pick up contacts with which they have no natural affinity. For instance, a person with any trace of Welsh, Cornish or Irish blood can pick up any of the Keltic contacts readily, including the Breton ones; the Highland Scottish are also open to him. He cannot, however, with equal ease pick up the Old Gods of the North, nor the primitive Etruscan gods of the South. On the other hand, a person of pure Nordic stock can pick up not only the Norse gods, but the Slavonic also. Moreover, owing to the fact that our culture is a Mediterranean culture, anyone who has been reared in its traditions, that is to say, who has had a classical education, can readily pick up the contacts of any of the Mediterranean faiths; the Grecian, Roman, Egyptian and Chaldean being equally accessible to him because they all interconnect with each other. The picking up of contacts, and the influence of places to that end, is a very interesting aspect of occult lore, and it will be seen that use is made of it in my novel. Up on the flanks of Snowdon, Murchison is at a disadvantage; he is not contacted with the native magnetism of the place; Brangwyn knows this, and when he wants to find a place in which Ursula and Murchison shall do the work he intends them to do, and make a magical marriage, he chooses the spot where Murchison, the less experienced of the two, shall have the advantage of the site, because he needs the extra force to bring him up to the necessary magnetic voltage and enable him to balance Ursula; she, being highly trained, will be able to adapt herself to the conditions. Consequently Brangwyn made an excuse to get rid of the Keltic hermitage and send Murchison off in search of a Nordic hermitage that would aid him in getting onto his own particular contacts. It will be remembered by those who are familiar with the pages of *The Winged Bull* that as soon as Murchison crossed the Humber when bringing the car from Wales, he felt as if he had 'come into his own.' The whole book, in fact is full of such touches as this, not put in deliberately, but coming out unconsciously, because I am not merely creating the world of the story, but living in it, and thus do those live and work who go after the deep things in occultism.

The scene of Astley's noisome abode is laid in north-east London because there are some very sinister spots round about that district;

others are to be found in Pimlico, and if I had known as much about occultism as I do now, Bayswater would not have been my first choice as a centre. Both Astley's and Brangwyn's temples were in the basements of their respective houses; those who are familiar with the history of the Mysteries will know that crypts and caves were always used for initiation ceremonies. Anyone who has had experience of underground working is well aware of the manner in which a cave or cellar will hold the magnetism as compared with a structure that is above ground. He will also know that a heavy, stone-built structure is much to be preferred to a flimsy one for magical purposes. Except for the temporary, meteoric flights of its charlatans, occultism is not a wealthy movement, and the Inner Light, in particular, starting from nothing and systematically making bricks without straw throughout its career, has not got the conditions for really powerful working, and it is wonderful what has been done in spite of the makeshifts that have had to be resorted to. When I look at the ruins of the temples of the great Fraternities of the past, I sometimes wonder whether the Inner Light will leave behind it any more imposing structures than the wooden huts at Glastonbury, or whether we shall have there our only memorial.

As I have already said, an epitome of the plot is not sufficient to enable the reader to understand this study of the real meaning of *The Winged Bull*; those who want to follow the explanations will need to re-read the book in order to see how the atmosphere builds up.

The story opens by revealing in a series of indirect touches the character and circumstances of Ted Murchison, the hero. It does not, as did the old-fashioned 'three-decker' novels, open with a series of solid chunks of description, history and moralising, nevertheless, the goods are delivered, and the reader, if he has eyes to see, is given the facts he needs to understand the causes behind what follows. If he has not got eyes to see, he will merely treat the story as a thriller, and a fanciful one at that. The method used resembles that of the Post-impressionist artist, who forces the observer to see a picture with an artist's eye if he is to see it at all; if he lacks all sense of line, composition and chiaroscuro, all he sees will be a series of disconnected dabs; co-ordination takes place subjectively. Likewise in the pages of *The Winged Bull* a quantity of stuff is pitchforked at the reader without explanation, and he is left to make what he can of it. On the surface, the book is an ordinary thriller, but beneath the surface there is the material in it to speak to the subconscious memory of the Mysteries, if one exists.

The scene opens outside the British Museum in a fog. Ted Murchison is represented as of that peculiar, and rather rare, type, who is by nature and inclination, a fighting man. Rare, that is to say, in its developed form in civilised cities; for being unadapted to the demands of city life, it is liable to take to crime in adolescence and spend its days in and out of prison; if more fortunately placed, it may succeed in getting out to the frontiers of Empire, where it does well. The Dominions are foolish to refuse men with a prison record, for they will find their best citizens among them. The hooligan from Borstal will often make good in the North-west Mounted Police.

Murchison had not actually taken to crime because he has been able to make his home with his brother, and therefore has not been absolutely desperate; but the uncongenial conditions and the enforced celibacy have taken their toll of him, embittering him and making him surly and uncouth. One of my critics said it was a pity I made the hero such an unpleasant character; but is he an unpleasant character? To my mind he is a tragic one. There is an old, and threadbare, saying, that to understand all is to forgive all, and this is a motif that appears frequently in my writings, a legacy, probably, from the days when I worked with nerve cases at a clinic. There one learnt to unravel the causes that gave rise to the conditions that appeared upon the surface as the general unsatisfactoriness of the neurotic. These, apart from the comparatively rare cases of bad heredity and endocrine unbalance, were to be found in the unnatural conditions of modern life due to the falsity of accepted values.

Of these unnatural conditions and falsifications of values the character of Murchison is put up as an example. He is good stuff mishandled; a temperament warped by thwarting; and the theme of the book turns very largely on the question of this mishandling of the stuff of life. Murchison is mishandled in one way, and Ursula in another. Murchison's mishandling is due to the all-pervading ignorance of the real nature of life; Ursula's to an abuse of that knowledge in unscrupulous hands such as Astley's; Brangwyn himself is the spokesman for what can be done by means of that knowledge when rightly used.

The representation of the hero of the story as a fighting man, and his contrasting with the pacifist and vegetarian Fouldes, the second villain, together with the Epicureanism of Brangwyn, is, I am afraid, a trailing of the tail of my coat before the idealists who form a large proportion of the ranks of the students of the occult, and of whom I have had a hearty sickener. So much mystical riff-raff has accumulated in the occult movement that in some of its aspects it is little more than a mutual admiration society of phenomenal foolishness, attracting what Kipling so aptly calls "The brittle intellectuals who snap beneath a strain." Every variety of lop-sided mind makes of it a happy hunting ground. I am far from saying that there is no truth and no virtue in any or all of the various ideals and 'isms' I have seen exploited, but it is characteristic of a lop-sided mind that in reacting to an admitted evil, it tries to stabilise the pendulum at the extreme of the opposite swing, and the remedy is worse than the disease. I have spent the better part of my life among cranks and idealists and reformers of one sort or another, and am pretty thoroughly disillusioned concerning all their ways and works; consequently my hero stands for normality and simplicity and common decency as against the high-falutingness of Fouldes which ends in a mess.

The background of Murchison is the suburban vicarage, and it is painted in pretty dark colours. The Rev. James Murchison is represented as sincere, narrow-minded, and doing infinite harm by his mishandling of life through ignorance and false values. He reduces his brother, a fundamentally decent man, to complete rebellion against all he stands for in life and religion. Murchison waxes blasphemous. He bids his brother's God go to His own Hell and stop there. He himself contemplates turning motor bandit. It has been a surprise to me that no reviewer, nor any of the correspondents that the book brought me, took exception to the blasphemies of Murchison. It speaks volumes for the state of public opinion that these can pass without comment. On the other hand, I put into the mouth of Brangwyn a defence of religion of a very peculiar kind; a defence of spiritual values against the life-destroying concepts that pass as religion at the present day. It is, in essence, an attack on the ascetic principle as being all wrong, a destruction of life values, with the Acton vicarage as an awful example of the result of putting orthodox precepts into practice with any degree of thoroughness.

The thesis of the book is found in the words: "Bring the Godhead down into manhood, and take the manhood up into godhead." The Kingdom of Heaven is to be sought in the normality of human life, not in any unnatural and far-fetched sainthood which is inevitably pathological because it is unnatural. Murchison has some rude things to say about cherubs that end at the neck in a little pair of wings.

The symbolism of the Winged Bull himself is explained pretty unequivocally in the course of the story. The bull has been, among all ages and races, the symbol of virile force. Winged like Pegasus and with a human head. I use him to represent the mental and spiritual aspect of sex in immediate association with its physical manifestation. Its magnetic side is also touched upon in the scene in the roof-garden where Ursula magnetises Murchison. In the earlier scene at the breakfast table, a hint is given as to the mode of operation of this force when Ursula fails to magnetise Murchison because she is not in emotional sympathy with him. An hour later, however, when her sympathy is aroused by remembering the debt that women owe to the fighting man, she is able to do then what she could not do before. Later again, in the final scene, after Ursula and Murchison have come together, the same motif recurs when, simply by sitting beside Ursula with his hand on her and in emotional sympathy with her, Murchison is filled with peace. These are all facts of sex psychology, and their significance is very little understood. Many marriages that pass for normal are totally unsatisfactory owing to the absence of this magnetic factor; and there are many relationships which are never consummated on the physical plane that are nevertheless deeply satisfying owing to its presence.

The message of the book concerns the spiritualising of sex. But not the spiritualising of sex by sublimating it onto other planes than the spiritual, but the spiritualising of sex by realising its profound spiritual significance and far-reaching psychological values.

It is not my wish to attack Christianity as a religion, but, when unsoftened by the sophistries of the confessional, its teaching on the subject of sex is about the most unsatisfactory thing that the wit of man has ever devised, and has made marriage as psychologically unhygienic as its indifference to the things of the flesh made the medieval towns physically insanitary. The unemptied cess-pools and airless houses of the Age of Faith have their psychological analogues in this so-called Age of Reason; for there are some things upon which we are still reluctant to use our reason, preferring, like the mediaeval burgher, to live with our filth rather than clear it out.

At such problems as these *The Winged Bull* runs a tilt in a tactful manner. A thesis is cut up into small pieces and scattered through the pages. It is not, I trust, too blatant, after the manner of the books that used to be inflicted on children on Sundays, wherein sticky lumps of piety filled out the exiguous plot. On the other hand, there is not a single reference, however casual, in its pages that is irrelevant; everything is an intrinsic part of the psychological picture. Take, for instance, the fact that the opening scene is laid in a fog. Is it introduced for mere scenic effect? Not at all. In a fog one is completely cut off from the sight of everything that reminds one of everyday life and holds one to one's normal personality; a fog is, consequently, very conducive to profound psychic experiences, and I have known several people who have had them in such circumstances. When, therefore, I wished to stage the scene of Murchison's break-through into the higher consciousness, I took him to the British Museum in a fog after a disappointment that had brought him to the end of his endurance. In the British Museum are relics of ancient faiths, highly charged with magical potency and giving off, even to this day, strong influences; a fog produces psychic receptivity, and the recoil from a devastating disappointment produces a highly charged emotional state; let it never be forgotten that emotions and magnetism are, for all practical purposes, synonymous terms in magic.

It is because my novels are packed with such things as these that I want my students to take them seriously. *The Mystical Qabalah* gives the theory, but the novels give the practice. Those who read the novels without having studied the Qabalah will get hints and a stimulus to their subconscious. Those who study the Qabalah without reading the novels will get an interesting intellectual jig-saw puzzle to play with; but those who study *The Mystical Qabalah* with the help of the novels get the keys of the Temple put into their hands. As Our Lord said: "Know ye not that your body is the temple of the Holy Ghost?"

⚛ Appendix 4 ⚛

ESTABLISHMENT OF THE SPHERE OF YESOD IN THE AURA

By DION FORTUNE

From the magical diary of Dion Fortune. Published in the "Inner Light Magazine", November 1931.

Monday, July 27ᵗʰ, 1931   *7.14 a.m*

FOR some time past I have been working on the symbol of the Tree of Life of the Qabalah, the diagram of the Ten Holy Emanations of God, by which the worlds were created, the basis of the Qabalistic system, which is one of the foundations of Western esotericism. It has occupied much of my time and attention, for I have been engaged in writing about it, and as I proceeded with my studies, I seemed to get more and more into its atmosphere, so that it was seldom absent from my mind.

I had always known that it was of primary importance as a meditation symbol, but at the time I went into my magical retirement I did not possess the necessary grades of initiation to avail myself of it, and during the last seven years all such deeper work had been deemed unadvisable. Now at last, I found myself in a position to open up the deeper aspects of my work, but had been so long in the Outer Court that I found I could not readily turn in and pass through the Veil.

Unconsciously to myself, however, the process had evidently been going on, and I found myself in my meditation beginning to abandon my usual methods in favour of work upon the Tree.

I will record the development and progress of this work, for it shows how I felt my way unconsciously along the lines of the system, for I had no conscious intention of making any practical use of it, being still turned outwards in my attention and interests.

I began by revising my knowledge of the Tree. It has a very intricate system of symbols assigned to each Path and Station, as those will know who have read my articles on the subject;[9] to these articles I must refer those of the readers of the present pages who are not already familiar with this subject, for I cannot explain the Tree or its principles in detail here, and must take much for granted for brevity's sake.

I recommenced my studies by reciting to myself each morning and evening the different primary correspondences of the Ten Holy Sephiroth. These are the Names of God assigned to each sphere, the archangels, the angels, and the planetary spheres. These I ran through in their order, the Deity Names, the archangels, the angels, etc. I did this for several days, thus becoming thoroughly fluent and familiar with the columns of strange-sounding words. This work was done in the ordinary consciousness, and so far as I am aware, no magical or psychic result whatsoever was produced.

Then I changed my method. I thought I knew the names well enough in their columns, and I would now learn them as associated with each Sephira. So instead of running through the series as I had done, I took all that was assigned to each Sephira and went through that.

Those who are familiar with the principles of Qabalism know that the Tree is not only associated with the sphere of the macrocosm, which is the universe, but also with the microcosm, which is man; and just as the Sephiroth are assigned to different planets in the macrocosm, so they are assigned to different spheres in the microcosm, the physical body of man; and there are methods of meditation which avail themselves of this, and form the Western analogue of the Hatha Yoga of the East. I knew of these systems, but had never used them myself for the reasons I have already given. Nor, in starting this method of meditation had I any intention of doing anything save rub up my rusty knowledge of the Tree and its symbolism.

As soon as I began to work through the symbols attached to each individual Sephira I found a change come over the spirit of my meditation, difficult to describe. Perhaps I can render it best by giving the details of my sensations at the time. I would be sitting in my accustomed chair, conscious of the sounds of the house, the

---

9 Subsequently published as *The Mystical Qabalah.*

touch of my clothes on my limbs, and all that makes up the sum-total of impressions that keep us in touch with the external world when the eyes are closed; then I would commence my mental rehearsal of the sacred names, and would suddenly find that I was aware of mental pictures only, to the entire exclusion of physical impressions. Nevertheless, I retained full co-ordination of consciousness, for I knew that I was conscious of the pictures, and that the physical impressions would return unless I maintained my concentration on the images rising in consciousness, and did not allow it to wander.

As soon as I thought over this experience later, in the light of subsequent developments, I realised that consciousness had been transferred from the dense body to the subtle body, and I had, without realising it, passed within the Veil, had passed from the objective to the subjective.

I went steadily down the Tree, reviewing Sephira after Sephira, conscious of power and a moving kaleidoscope of mind-pictures, deeply sunken in meditation, oblivious of my physical body and its sensations, till I came to the Sephira Yesod. As I rehearsed the Divine Names associated with this sphere, a picture suddenly formed in consciousness, at first as if seen through a window, and then as if I stood in the midst of it. The scene was a sandy desert by moonlight; at my feet a lake or inland sea rippled against the sand; a few scattered palm-trees were on my left, a little behind me, and on my right, in the middle distance, a string of camels moved slowly away. For quite a while I contemplated this scene, and it grew in reality moment by moment as I gazed. I could absolutely hear the wash of the calm water as it lapped the sand and see the flash of the moonlight reflected from the ripples.

In the far distance, across the water, I could see dimly the white walls of a city, its round white domes dominating it, all still and asleep in the moonlight.

Then as I stood and listened, a change occurred. Out of the sky over the water a vast angelic figure began to form, and I saw what I felt to be an archangel bent above me in a vast curve, crescent-shaped. The colouring was all in moonlight greys and misty mauves and blues, in keeping with the dim yet luminous scene. The face was calm and still, not so much sad as absolutely unsmiling, and very intent. This vast being leaned towards me and showed me a symbol which he held in his hand. I had some difficulty in making out what it was, but he persisted, and finally I saw it to be a slender cone of white plaster, point upwards, which in some way I associated with the round white domes of the distant city. It seemed to be made of the same material.

It seemed as if the vision would have persisted indefinitely, but the meditation time drew to a close, and I performed the usual formula of the closing of the Veil, and withdrew.

But as I completed the first stage of the withdrawal, that is to say, as I visualised myself entering the purple disc of Yesod on my diagram, I felt a strange sensation; I seemed to vibrate backwards and forwards between the objective and the subjective like a shuttle; the purple disc of Yesod appeared to come off the chart, to expand in size, and to be within my aura. For a moment I shuttled backwards and forwards between the symbol through which I had re-entered the objective plane and my own body; I seemed to have got an objectified disc of Yesod in my aura, and did not quite know where to put it.

I knew that to Yesod were assigned the Sphere of the Moon in the macrocosm, and the basal portion of the trunk in the microcosm, and I could not make out whether I should wear my purple disc before or behind, so I tried it on both ways in that vivid pictorial imagination of deliberately induced vision. It seemed to me at first that it ought to be pictured over the adrenals, where Kundalini is coiled. I tried it there, but it did not seem right. Then I tried it in front, but that was even worse.

Then, for some unknown reason, the sphere itself took charge, and seemed to slide right inside the physical body till it took up its position resting upon the floor of the pelvis, just in front of the spine, and reaching upwards to the level of the lowest ribs. I was exceedingly conscious of this disc of quivering purple light in this position, and also of the appearance of my own skeleton, and the sense of the objective reality of this disc still remains with me, in marked distinction from the rest of the Sephiroth which have not been thus magically formulated.

The following day I proceeded to look up the symbolism of Yesod and see how far the vision was true to type. I am pretty familiar with the symbolism of the Tree, for I have frequent occasion to refer to it, but I could not, from memory, have run through all the minor associations of Yesod. It is interesting to note, therefore, the extent to which the vision made use of them, gathering them from my subconscious mind, or in some cases apparently from the racial subconscious concerning which Jung has so much that is valuable to tell us.

Yesod is the Sphere of the Moon, and its sephirothic colours are indigo, violet, dark purple, and yellowish green flecked with azure. Gabriel is the archangel associated with the moon, and he is the regent of the West, the quarter associated with the element of water. It will be remembered that water played an important part in my vision.

But the moon has another association on the Tree as well as that of Yesod. It is associated with the Thirteenth Path which unites Kether with Tiphareth. With this Path is also associated the letter Gimel of the Hebrew alphabet. The meaning of Gimel is Camel. We now see the significance of several symbols in the vision.

The Sephirothic colours associated with the Thirteenth Path are blue, silver, cold pale blue, and silver rayed sky-blue. It will be remembered that the vision was confined exclusively to the colours of blue, purple and grey.

In the symbolism of the Tree as applied to the microcosm, Yesod corresponds with the generative organs. The Moon, the sphere of Yesod in Assiah, (the physical world), also corresponds to Diana, who presides over childbirth. It is obvious, therefore, that we should expect to find life symbolism somewhere in the vision. The only trace I can find of it is in the curious cone-shaped symbol in the hand of the angel; this, it will be remembered was associated by me with the white domes of the far city, dimly seen. This association, however, is from consciousness, and does not evoke the assent of subconsciousness; but this, of course, may be due to the inhibitions of the censor, as was my difficulty in making out the nature of the symbol that the angel was showing me; the palm also is a fecundity symbol. It is interesting to note that the Thirty-second Path from Malkuth to Yesod is associated with the skeleton, and it will be remembered that I saw my own skeleton very clearly.

The whole vision then, may be taken as a glyph of the sphere of Yesod, embracing the moon symbolism and that of its presiding archangel, rapidly thrown together into a cartoon by the subconscious mind. I may say that it took me very much longer to look up the symbolism and verify it than it did for the vision to formulate itself to the inner eye.

Finally we may ask ourselves, what was the result of the vision, and its practical value, if any? The result was the apparently permanent formulation of the purple disc of Yesod in my pelvis. I had always understood that these centres formed in the aura, not the physical body, hence my surprise when the sphere interiorised itself. I had a year previously had a similar experience on the Thirty-second Path, the Path of Saturn, which connects Malkuth with Yesod, and had there experienced a curious sense of objective reality, and seen a vision of the Great One of the Night of Time, with his reaping-hook and hour-glass. Ever since then I have had a peculiar sense of familiarity and security upon that Path, usually considered so difficult and dark.

The full result of my experience in Yesod remains to be seen, but I imagine it will give me the same sense of familiarity, security and reality that I received after I had been through the experiment I have described on the Path of Saturn. It is very clear to me, that a Path on which one has had such an experience as I have described is entirely different henceforward to a Path on which one has not experienced this curious vision which 'comes alive' and assumed objective reality.

~⚬ Appendix 5 ⚬~

NOTES ON 'THE CIRCUIT OF FORCE'

By DION FORTUNE

From a Society of the Inner Light source, c.1939

OF the four Elements in Malkuth two are active, a subtle and a dense, and two are passive, a subtle and a dense. This gives rise to "Alternating Polarity", a marriage being a matter of four quarters, not two halves.

A natural attitude to relationships will ensure a correct tidal flow of force. An incorrect attitude leads to congestion or starvation of force. Since a return to nature is rarely socially acceptable, ritual may prove to be an effective corrective – at least better than nothing.

The personality receives energy from two sources, spiritual energy via the mind and elemental energy via the etheric. The physical body is not involved in this for it obtains its energy from food and drink. But bodily posture can determine the nature of the energy-flow.

The energy out of which the etheric double is organised is elemental energy and it appears to flow in a circuit round the Earth.

There is a pulsation, a rhythmic ebb and flow in the subtle bodies which is readily susceptible to regulation by the mind.

This influence is not by the will but by the subconscious mind which is in turn influenced by the imagination. Care is needed in the exercise of this regulation because the dividing line between control of the etheric and disruption of the automatic processes of the physical body is extremely narrow.

In the human being the main current of force corresponds with the centre line of the body.

The human being can be said to consist of a physical body, a subtle body, a mental body and a spiritual nucleus. The spiritual nucleus seems to be the channel of a limitless supply of energy from the Unmanifest.

The other bodies derive their pabulum from the substance of their respective levels. It is important to distinguish between the substance of a plane, and dynamic energy.

The etheric double is the link between mind and matter.

The input of elemental earth energy is not through the feet but via Malkuth and it is transferred to Yesod and there transformed from universal energy to personal energy or magnetism.

In this way the impersonal vitality of the earth is transformed into very personal sex force.

This force is carried up to the higher centres of man in ritual – by sublimation. If the mind control fails, sexual imagery can arise; yet without this personal dynamism it is not possible to work an effective ceremony.

The centres always work in pairs; for instance, Malkuth supplies the force for Yesod; Yesod supplies the motive power for Tiphareth.

The subtle magnetism in humans is as much mental as physical; when an aura impinges on aura there is an interchange of force bringing harmony. When two people are associated exclusively over a period equilibrium is reached and there is no 'spark'.

Refreshment may be found via a new terminal but this does not imply a liaison, ordinary social intercourse will suffice; this indicates that reserves of a person's own magnetism are released by imagination.

Some say that all magnetism is subjectively stored and emotionally released; others, that energy is derived either from the Unmanifest or the Earthsoul. Probably both are the case, and it is best to use both subjective and impersonal cosmic sources together.

The subjective technique is to use auto-suggestion through the imagination. The impersonal technique is to use dramatisation through ritual.

Mind cannot master matter by direct action. The etheric double is the key and it is influenced by concentration and the image-making faculty of the mind. This is how energy is directed to higher levels.

If the control is imperfect there may be a stimulus to the passions. Sex is a function, not an emotion; it cannot be banished but it can be directed. There is no such thing as sex *per se*, it is life force manifesting on a particular level. Orgasm earths the force; so does a properly worked magical ceremony.

Occult ceremonial uses magnetic force, concentrated and under control, as the raw material from which the higher forces are sublimated.

The main channels of sublimation are art and religion, and each has a contribution to make. Sublimation provides an outlet and the return flow is from all sorts of relationships; a return is available cosmically – Pan or Isis will return a polarising ray of energy as much as a personal relationship.

Capacity to polarise does not depend on sympathy or agreement but on type. The Principle of Polarity lies in reciprocal relationship.

There is objective and subjective polarity and it is probable that the objective arises through magnetic induction from the subjective, not vice versa. If mind comes before matter, subjective conditions are the causes of objective circuits of force. Thus the condition of our higher levels may set up magnetic fields and put us in touch with objective fields of force.

Although we can only influence these higher levels indirectly, the initiatives of our conscious lower levels open the way for the higher consciousness. The consequent impulse to regulate our conduct with regard to principle is such an example of polarity, and such self-polarisation is the basis of all deliberate induction and control of the circuit of force.

The higher levels polarise with cosmic forces by means of meditation and realisation through the Daath centre. Lower levels make contact with the elemental forces through the aura by means of Yoga practices in individual cases and by means of ceremonial with groups.

Relative potency is not static or 'fixed', dependent on form, but on 'voltage' or vitality. Moreover the exchange is always alternating, never a permanent one-way flow. And the exchange can be between the parts and the whole as well as between 'opposites'.

ᵜ Appendix 6 ᵜ

INNER PLANE TEACHING ON POLARITY

DECEMBER 16th 1940

Trance address via Dion Fortune to eight senior members of the Society of the Inner Light, December 16ᵗʰ 1940

I have told you there must be privacy and freedom in your individual lives, but equally you will find in all magical work that nobody can work alone, and according to the work you want to do you will work in polarity, or triangle or circle. For the formation of such a group, the first consideration is atmosphere – to be in harmony with the people you work with, for you cannot do practical occult work unless you have happy conditions. You may have to wait a long time; for magical working must be as balanced as a choir.

In circle work you will get the best results if you have a balanced proportion of the sexes. Never have a greater proportion than two to one of the negative factor to the positive, otherwise your work becomes unduly negative. Polarity is the key to all magical work. Even in circle working you always get one to sit opposite the leader of the circle, and unless the leader finds a suitable person, the force will not start to flow. He must have capacity and understanding on the matter in hand, and once the flow begins between the leader and one person, it starts the current of force in circuit.

The principle of polarity is of special importance. It is one of the basic principles. Polarity means the function of flow and return of force. It is not fixed. It is an alternating current and therefore constantly changing. Sometimes one or another is negative. For certain types of polarity work you have the relation of teacher and pupil. I want to explain to you carefully the difference between polarity work between equals and polarity between superiors and inferiors. In polarity work between superiors and inferiors, (of course I refer to grades), polarity is fixed and cannot be reversed. Therefore when the need comes for reversal, you change partners – the superior of the pair works with an equal, and the inferior finds another equal. Now the superior who has been positive works as negative to his equal, and the inferior works as positive to his equal. Is that clear?

You must have alternating polarity periodically, otherwise, if fixed too long, you cease to be magnetic to each other. Now let me illustrate this. First, you have seen how your leader seeks contact with persons outside your group. It is for the sake of reversal of polarity, and as she finds someone who is equal and to whom she can be negative, so she becomes re-magnetised. She will always seek re-polarisation from external contacts, and she will polarise on a particular facet. This means that you take a person and pick out one particular quality – one facet on which they are superior, and work on that aspect only – all other aspects being inhibited. This is an important point in practical work for it enables you to work with a wide range of experience. There are few you can accept unreservedly to polarise with completely; it is asking too much of human nature.

So each one of you will polarise with this or that person – with this or that quality according to the knowledge they possess. The personal union on which the once-born pin their hopes is unworkable in magic, so don't attempt it.

[In answer to a question on polarity. If two are working, whether a third is present.]
Not necessarily. Polarity of the two is a specific thing, and you would not get a third. There is, however, one behind each of the pairs so that you get a double polarity – positive and negative on the inner, and positive and negative on the outer. There is the priest who represents Pan and the priestess who represents Isis. Then, when you are working a rite you get the other pair – the High Priest and the Lector – the pair of form as well as the pair of force. You always have two bringing through power and two building the forms. Two initiates of the Ancient Mysteries co-operating with the High Priest and Lector. Polarity working is the basis of all other forms of group magic, and all others forms are extensions of it.

131

I am giving you principles, not the practical application. If you can grasp them and ask questions, you will be answered, but if you do not grasp them, I do not put dangerous tools into your keeping.

[In answer to a question on mystical polarity.]
It runs through the whole of life. Misunderstanding of it is the cause of many difficulties among organisations of all kinds. Right handling of it is the inspiration of all leadership. In mystical work the contact is on the Inner Planes. It is between the devotee and the Deity – in adoration. But some form of polarisation is essential to all personalities, but it need not be with persons of the opposite sex. Certain magical work does depend on this, not on physical sex as such, but because the vehicles of a man or woman are better suited to carry certain voltages. A woman can work with a woman, and a man with a man, but it is seldom as satisfactory as a man working with a woman, although your leader was initiated by a female Guru.

Another point arising out of what we have been saying is that a soul is bi-sexual – both aspects are present in the higher self, and the personality forms the two poles of the magnet, and according to which pole is inserted into the physical body in incarnation, will be the sex thereof. When you develop, you come to the point where both aspects are functional in consciousness, and then you get a man with much of the woman in him and a woman with much of the man. In certain anomalies you see these things, but they are quite different from the developed adept.

In the undeveloped person one aspect only is developed. In the anomaly, one is repressed and the other developed at its expense. But in the adept, the second aspect is developed until it matches the primary. You see the difference?

Occasionally you get a type of man, the kind tied to his mother's apron strings, and there the male aspect has been repressed; but frequently you get women in whom the female aspect is repressed and they are masculine in mind and often in body. A very important part of the knowledge of occult work and human relationships lies in the law of alternating polarity and the re-magnetising of each other. You can establish relationships with many different types by dissecting out a given quality in a person. These are important clues to practical work. And remember, you need to exchange polarity with anyone you are working with regularly in order to get the best results. You also need to have polarity with many different persons for full development of experience and function.

You can get exchange of magnetism between two of the same sex, but the trouble is that the flow thus exchanged cannot flow in circuit. Let us put it this way: The flow and return in a pipe is like a normal magnetic relationship. With two of the same sex, each one has half the pipe and they are not joined up. It is this leakage of magnetism that makes it dangerous, for, from the magnetism thus discharged, certain elemental forms are built up. The same applies to auto-sexuality. In ancient days these methods were used for ritual purposes. We do not propose to use them as great difficulties and dangers would be involved, but under certain circumstances auto-sexuality can be used as a means of drawing off magnetism through magical images.

[In answer to another question on mystical polarity.]
You can work in mystical polarity without knowledge of magic, but if you work with magic you must also have knowledge of mysticism, and on another occasion I will give teaching concerning this. Magic and mysticism are not mutually exclusive; they are both legitimate methods.

Well now, continuing the matters I have spoken of, if you observe the working of all the rites you have seen, you will note how polarity is carried out. The positive and negative maintained – a man and woman opposite each other when possible. Now when it comes to the practical work, the same principle prevails, and as I told you before, you will all in turn get the opportunity of the experience of all aspects of the work as they are built up and made available. Your leader has first to get the archetypal ideas. Then give them form on the physical plane, and when that has been done they are available for everybody. Now when she is doing that she works by the law of polarity. First she will have negative relations with whoever on the Inner Planes is the Master concerned, in which he gives, and she receives. Then she reverses and works with someone on the physical plane. She gives and he receives, and in order to achieve that reversal, she usually works with a man; and she has worked with various men, some you know, and some you don't, and she will always do so. In the days when her husband afforded her protection there were no difficulties, but now that protection is withdrawn it must be afforded her by the group. She must be able to work thus without being exposed to scandalous tongues, therefore, the wisdom and protection of the group must serve to guard her, just as the bees in a hive guard the queen bee – the layer of eggs – the one creature in the hive that can lay eggs. That is why group formation is essential for the work so as to make conditions and give the necessary protection.

Now, my son, the priest, you had experience of the work for several years. Did it ever give rise to scandal? *[Answer: Never]*

Was there ever anything in that relationship that could have justified scandal? *[Answer: Nothing]*

When that phase of work was finished, were you left uncompensated? *[Answer: No, I was fully compensated]*

There you have his testimony. Since then, your leader worked with another priest. The relationship served its purpose, fulfilled its end – gave her what was needed and ended, but the priest has not been left uncompensated, nor will be.

Now a third priest works in a third relationship, and I would ask you to assist and protect that work, for it is necessary for bringing through the teaching, and he who receives it passes it on again, not to one, but to all. And in asking you to assist in that work by making a circle of protection around it, I give you my assurance there is nothing in that relationship to cause scandal or bring disgrace upon the work. It is a magical relationship. For that it is necessary that persons should be in sympathy, but as I told you before, the personal factor does not come into it.

I have exemplified three cases of polarity in which your priestess has been used, representing the three Rays of this Fraternity; in each case the work was undertaken as work. Personal relationships had to build up to enable the work to be done, but in each case the relationship was entered upon for the work and not for personal ends. These matters are entirely to do with the inner work of the Temple. There is nothing personal in them, but it is not easy for people to understand who have not known the impersonality of Temple work.

⏤᷁ Appendix 7 ᷁⏥

RECOMMENDED READING

The Winged Bull – Dion Fortune – Weiser Books
The Goat-Foot God – Dion Fortune – Weiser Books
The Sea Priestess – Dion Fortune – Weiser Books
Moon Magic – Dion Fortune – Weiser Books
The Mystical Qabalah – Dion Fortune – Weiser Books
The Occult Fiction of Dion Fortune – Gareth Knight – Thoth
    Publications
The Circuit of Force – Dion Fortune & Gareth Knight – Thoth
    Publications
An Introduction to Ritual Magic – Dion Fortune & Gareth Knight –
    Thoth Publications
Dion Fortune and the Inner Light – Gareth Knight – Thoth
    Publications
Magic and the Power of the Goddess – Gareth Knight – Destiny Books

⌁ INDEX ⌁

Index